Incredibly

EASY SUCCESS

PRINCIPLES

MAKE YOUR LIFE WONDERFUL!

Norene Thomas-Davoren

1

INCREDIBLY EASY SUCCESS PRINCIPLES
Make Your Life Wonderful

Printed in the United States of America
Edited by Ida Vallo Morris
First Printing: June 2016
Library of Congress Control Number: 2016942468
ISBN-13: 978-1-944917-01-2—ISBN-10: 1-944917-01-2

AARK House Publishing

www.AARKHousePublishing.com

Dedications

This book is dedicated to the most precious two women that ever graced the face of this earth. They are my mother, Ludie White, Thomas, Ridges and my godmother, Mateldia Goodrich. Both of these precious jewels instilled deep into me that anything is possible; that all I had to do was:

- Trust in God
- Get a Good Education
- Don't Forget to Pray
- Thank God for His Blessings
- Work Hard
- Be Honest
- Treat People Fairly
- Have Integrity
- Stay Focused

Life is Wonderful. So are you.

Contents

Introduction

"We all strive to be kind and loving to our friends, co-workers, and family. Why can't we be just as kind and loving to ourselves, and work toward our own dreams and goals?"

~ Norene Thomas,
Coach, Motivational Public Speaker, Registered Nurse and Author

---

We all have areas in which we want to improve and be more successful. For some, it is improving our careers or realizing our dream as a thriving entrepreneur. For others, it may be improving how we deal with people or being more loving to family and friends, or even just finding a mate. We may want to become successful financially. Whatever it is, certain principles hold true for achieving success – no matter what area we are striving for. These principles will work. Happily, I have set these principles out for you in an easy to read and follow fashion.

These principles are simple and, like all simple truths, powerful. If you apply the principles in this book to whatever it is you want to achieve, you WILL achieve your goal, more. This is a fantastic reality. We are not placed on this earth to NOT achieve our goals. We are not meant to suffer. We are meant to shine, be prosperous, and love our lives. And, to accomplish that, we only have to be willing to do the work and stay the course in order to achieve what it is we want.

The following work/principles are not difficult. In fact, they're fun and easy to implement. Your life will expand, your capacity for joy will expand, and your sense of self-esteem and respect for others will expand.

So why do I feel I am someone who can help you, and why do I even see myself as an expert? First, I have trained with the best. Specifically, with Jack Canfield, author of The Chicken Soup Book series and many other books, in how to help people achieve their goals, and help them get to where they want to be. But even before that, I went through all the difficulties you may have gone through, or perhaps are going through – a childhood without money, several businesses that succeeded then failed, a failed marriage and life as a single mom – however, I managed to persevere and not give up and overcome all these to live the life I so desired.

How did I do this? Through living and staying true to my values, and by applying the principles in this book. That's why I want to share them with you. They work!

Here's a little of my own story, and how these principles that I am going to share with you ended up changing my own life: I was born in Bennettsville, South Carolina, a very small town where everyone knew everyone. We were nine children, and I was the youngest of the first 7. My father died when I was two years old, so I was literally raised by a single mom until I was around 14, when my mom remarried a wonderful man. This man was a good father to us but he also struggled hard financially. From this union, I was blessed with two younger brothers, "Slim" Calvin and Warren. Even though they're younger, they are like my older brothers. They are still protective of me and extremely encouraging to me in my own drive to succeed. They are my rock. We were, as you can see, a big family, and not one with a lot of extra cash, but we were very close knit. We owe all of this to my mom, who made the ultimate sacrifice of keeping us all together and raising this big family, especially when our house burned to the ground and it was even harder financially. Yet she still kept us all together.

Hers was not an easy life. She worked hard cooking hot lunches in the school and did domestic work. My step father was a farmer and we lived on the farm, picking cotton, and raising chickens, cattle, pigs, and even growing our own fruits and vegetables in order to make ends meet. All of us worked.

But as hard as life was, we were raised with values that have guided me throughout my life. My mother taught us that our name was everything, and not to do anything that would cause us shame. We were a proud family, taught to always look good, go to church, especially Sunday school, and she wanted us either to be in the choir or the usher board. She taught us to be close to one another, with a philosophy that if one of us hurt, then we all hurt. If one was in need, then we all had the responsibility to help the other. I always describe my childhood as "Little money. Lots of love."

Yet, much as I loved my family, I did not see myself staying in South Carolina. One day I realized I was just tired of going nowhere fast, tired of being broke, tired of not getting a job, tired of not being able to do the things I knew I was capable of doing. I was just tired of being tired.

It was a case, as we all know, of nothing from nothing can lead to nothing. I wanted to change that formula for myself and my family, especially my mother who had always worked so hard to keep a roof over our heads and food on the table. And there were many times she didn't know how she was going to make it, or even what we would have for dinner.

My mom was old school but very relevant for today, since she believed in one of our most important principles, "Always take 100% responsibility for everything." My mom taught us always to dream and to dream big. Well, I dreamed of becoming a nurse, but I delayed it based on naysayers saying that you had to be at the top of the class in science and math to become a nurse. Those two classes were not my strong suit. So I put nursing on hold for many, many years until I realized a very dear friend of mine was getting her bachelor's in nursing. She was not a "rocket scientist," so, after all, I could do it, too!

9

Before that, I did go off to Clinton Community College to study Business Administration and, to my surprise, there I became an A student. That just goes to show you never really know where or when you are going to excel. An environment can change everything. In one place you may be mediocre, another place you are a leader. So don't get down about what is not working, because something else will.

After college I went to New York, where I knew there was more opportunity for me. I started working in a factory and I worked there a year or so, while living with my Uncle Slim and Aunt Mary in Englewood, New Jersey. But I had traveled far, just so I could be on my own, so I had a plan to get my own place. Soon I had saved enough money to rent a room in Brooklyn, where I continued working in the factory. I tried to find office work but I wasn't successful. Everyone said I didn't have enough experience.

This led me back to school. I went to Katherine Gibbs Secretarial School. Gibbs graduates were very popular with employers at that time because "Everyone wanted a Gibbs' Girl." Even before I graduated, I landed a job as a secretary at The Nestle Company and worked there for many years. In fact, I thought I would retire from there. However, as fate had it, the division I worked in was sold off and I had the opportunity to move to Pennsylvania with the new company or accept their severance package. They gave me a generous severance, which afforded me the opportunity to pursue my lifelong dream of becoming a nurse.

The road was long and hard and the money got short along the way. My girlfriend and I would share yogurt and an apple for lunch. We always told everyone we were on a diet. Needless to say, we had no money for lunches.

At 29, I achieved my first dream. So what does that tell us? Never give up on your dream. It's waiting for you to make it come true, and it doesn't matter when you finally get to it.

What's important is that you get to it.

During this time, I had also married my second husband, who is an extremely wonderful and supportive husband. We had another child. I was working full time and raising my children. This was not easy, but where there is a will, there is a way.

Once I graduated as a Licensed Practical Nurse, I worked in the Laguardia Hospital and at Rikers Island Prison in the infirmary. I did see, at the hospital, that LPNs did not get the same recognition as the RNs so I decided to go back to school and become an RN. I attended Edna McConnell Clark School of Nursing, a division of Columbia University, and graduated as an RN.

My career at Rikers lasted many, many years. I retired as an onsite Director of Nursing in 2006, and am still working twice a week for them, as a consultant.

I did many things along the way to make ends meet; I was a Parking Enforcer, (Meter Maid) for the City of New York. While there I met a marvelous woman for whom I became a driver, she inspired and encouraged me so very much. This lady was Matilda Goodrich; she became my godmother. I *was* also an Executive Secretary for the Nestlé company for many years. Until they sold off the water division, at that point I decided to leave and to peruse my lifelong dream nursing. I studied nursing. After I chose to leave Nestlé's.

I wanted to open a daycare business, which I knew quite a bit about, just by the nature of my own child needing day care. I worked hard, keeping my eyes on the prize and finally my dream was realized. However, as time passed, I ran into financial hardship.

I was afraid to ask for help, but I knew I had no other choice or I would lose my business. This same woman for whom I had been a driver came to my rescue and sent me -- in the overnight mail, no less -- the

11

amount I was asking for, along with three blank checks for when, or if, I needed more.

She showed me that we all need help to accomplish our dreams and we have to have the humility and graciousness to accept help. And just as importantly, I learned that we have to have the courage and nerve to tell people what we need. "Just ask," became my motto. You can't get help unless people know you need it and want it.

My daycare business in Queens, New York, did well for nine years. I was then offered an On-Site directorship at Rikers and, with its benefits and stability, I decided to take that route. I closed the business and went onto the new. What did that teach me? That when things get stale, we have to go with the flow of new opportunities. Be open. Be curious. And say "yes" to situations that may have better results for us.

My daycare business had a great location (always important), which didn't require advertising (a great savings for us), but it had a ceiling on its potential (just by the nature of the neighborhood) and so I decided to explore other venues.

I decided while working at Rikers I would start a different business, Wound Care, a seminar business on how to prevent, treat and manage wounds. I was certified in this area and I knew in my heart, as I had known I was meant to be a nurse, that I was also meant to give seminars. It seemed intelligent to blend my nursing skills and my speaking skills. What I call sticking to one's core genius when making a change.

I went into business with high hopes and great expectations but, as life will have it, was met with many unforeseen obstacles.

But even so, I retired from Rikers and, as I mentioned, went on to consult there. My life was good, happy in a long and stable second marriage, and I was ready to devote myself to something new and

12

meaningful. What is new and meaningful to me is sharing with others all the lessons I have learned in the various businesses I have grown and learned from.

In these days of difficult economic times regarding jobs and sometimes non-existent pensions, I can help you with reinvention, something many of us need and want now. I can share with you how to be happy at what you do and how to go from where you are to where you want to be.

We all strive to be kind and loving to our friends and family, so why can't we be just as kind and loving to ourselves and our own dreams? Who you are, what strengths and talents you have, what values you bring into the world...these are your gifts to share. You know in your heart what you would like for yourself. You may not want to believe in its possibility, but the dream is there, and very much alive.

Well, I say believe in it and know you can achieve it. Just follow these 12 principles and watch your life grow into what you long for, beyond your wildest imagination.

"We are what we repeatedly do. Excellence is not an act but a habit."

Make these principles your habit and you are sure to achieve success.

~ Aristotle, Greek philosopher

The Secrets of
Proven Success
Will Surprise You

*"Our talents are unique to us and we owe it to ourselves to explore
and make something of them to contribute to the world."*

~ Norene Thomas

---

*"Success is not the key to happiness. Happiness is the key to success.
If you love what you are doing, you will be successful."*

~ Albert Schweitzer, German theologian, philosopher and physician who
received the Nobel Peace Prize in 1952 for his philosophy of "Reverence for
Life."

Before we begin discussing the principles of success, let's set some
ground rules. Here are some quick thoughts to put in your mind before
we go into the principles themselves. These are truths that every
successful person knows and they are your platform for success. So
let's take a quick look at these little secrets and then we will go on to
the principles.

**You don't have to be an "A" student in school. And you don't have to
be young.**

(Just determined.)

15

Being old is an honor. I graduated Magna Cum Laude with my Bachelor's in Health Service Administration after I was 50 years old. And I earned my Master's in Health Services Administration even later in life. No excuses.

Most of us have been told that where we go to college and what we learn in college is a precursor to our success. But that's not always a fact. Of course, many Harvard lawyers do extremely well and many people are fast tracked to their success through schooling. But, fascinatingly, most successful people seem to make it through hard work, and positive and inventive thinking in the areas they are passionate about. Not through pedigree.

Famously, Steve Jobs, Bill Gates, Hemingway, and many others did not complete or attend college. Jay Z and Tyler Perry did not finish high school, and look how far they have gone! Folorunsho Alakija is a Nigerian businesswoman who is the second richest African woman, after Isabel Dos Santos. She began her career as an executive secretary, having never gone to college, although she did study fashion design at the American College, London and the Central School of Fashion. She started a tailoring company called Supreme Stitches. It rose to prominence and fame within a few years, and as Rose of Sharon House of Fashion, became a household name.

Often, people who do not finish college are more driven to improve themselves in the real world, are more fascinated by a variety of things and give themselves permission to experiment with life to find

16

out what is really right for them. Perseverance and drive lead to success, not just one's education.

The other surprise is that even living, as we do, in a youth culture, we don't have to be young to become successful. Many successful people came to it older. Roy Crock of McDonald's fame was in his 50s, after first creating some fast food items that no one wanted. Once he figured out the Big Mac, all bets were off on his success. Alberta Hunter, the jazz singer, became a nurse at 62 and a famous performer, awarded at the Kennedy Center, at 82. Colonel Sanders became successful in his 60s, after having been a steam engine stoker, insurance salesman, and filling station operator. He began selling fried chicken from his roadside restaurant in North Corbin, Kentucky, during the great depression. He saw the potential for restaurant franchising and the first KFC franchise opened in Utah in 1952. Many people became financially successful turning over real estate in their 50s and even older. Jack Cover invented the Taser when he was in his 60s. Point being, it ain't over till it's over, and one should not focus on age but on what one can contribute to the world. So, if you are older or younger, the same principles apply: Hard work and inventive thinking will get you to where you want to be.

You need values.

It's true that some not very nice people have become successful. But, for success to last and to feel good, you need to be living by your values. You need to be good to your family and friends. You need to honor your commitments. You need to be aware of how you can help those around you. You need to do a little bit each day toward what you

17

value (be it a garden, a grandchild, writing a novel, helping someone or people in general), and making that part of your life count. If you do that, you will be in the frame of mind to attract success, and people will want to be around you. If that is the case, new opportunities and new ways of seeing opportunities will open up to you. But you will only give off the clarity and healthiness that other people will want to be associated with if you are living by strong and honorable values.

Your dreams will guide you.

Probably when you were young, you had dreams. I don't mean the passing ones, like becoming a movie star or President of the United States. I mean the ones that were particular to your talents and close to your heart. You might have dreamed that you always wanted to teach or live in Thailand or help people in disaster zones or be an entrepreneur, life coach, or write a memoir. Whatever it was that stuck in your brain and heart and would not go away, is something you should be doing.

Our talents are unique to us and we owe it to ourselves to explore those and make something of them to contribute to the world. If you're not sure about what exactly is your venue to be successful, meditate on a place that is meaningful to you and then think about what you told yourself you wanted to do with your life when you were young and what you tell yourself now. That is a guiding light. If you secretly dream of marriage or working with young children, or being a life coach, a school teacher, a businessman/woman, then heed your dreams. They know the real you.

You have to stop complaining.

Complaining is a very strong indicator that you are dissatisfied about something. Therefore, in order to get to where you want to go, stop the blame game. Complaining cannot and should not be a part of your success plan. Because usually the things we complain about are things we can change. For example: you want a better job – go where the jobs are. You want to eat healthier, learn to cook healthier, or take a cooking class. The list could go on.

Most of the time when we complain it is to the wrong person. The one that cannot help us. For example, you complain to your spouse about your coworker or about your boss. Successful people learn to take complaints and turn them into their desired outcomes. So can you, if you stop complaining about what if and concentrate on what is.

Be willing to change.

You won't be successful doing what you've always done and expecting a different outcome. You will have to change something to get a different result. It might be where you live, how you spend your time, or even a part of your personality or your friends. You will have to get out there and make new connections. It will be scary, but nobody can know about you if you're always at home. You have to be willing to identify where you need to change and be willing to be uncomfortable while you try it. You have to be open to the new. Change is usually good, your mind becomes stimulated, you learn new ways of doing things, you increase your opportunities. You find you like doing things you did not even know existed. You meet new people and they open your mind with their ideas. If you are seeking success in love or

19

finances or in work, you have to clear the runway for your success. You have to acquire success principles and put them into action. Change is scarier in the abstract, the actual changing is usually quite fun and will make you proud of yourself. In short, you are going to find that change leads to encouragement, empowerment and self-esteem. You'll take on activities and discover talents you never knew you had.

There will be tough times but they can be temporary.
Every successful person has taken a lot of rejection, and has failed at numerous things. Nobody has a perfect track record and if a person hasn't experienced any failure, they are not taking enough risks. (I exclude surgeons from this topic.) But even surgeons, when becoming surgeons, made mistakes. Being a nurse, I know they can take out the wrong kidney or cut the wrong foot! There is always a struggle in life, especially when you are working toward what you really want. However, when you get rejected or things don't work out quite the way you want, that is not the end of the story. It just means you have to keep going and look for a new opportunity.

As an example, you may lose your job only to discover that you will find a new life that suits you much better in a different job or by life leading you to live in a new place. You may lose your boyfriend/girlfriend only to meet a man or woman much more loving and committed and kind. You may lose a backer for a venture you are involved in, only to have that same person come in a year or so later. We don't know what the future holds, but we do know that life is continually regenerating and that successful people are not daunted

20

by tough times. They see tough times as a challenge and go back to the drawing board to find another way to accomplish their goals. As the Chinese say, perseverance furthers.

You'll need help along the way.

"No man is an island... No one can stand alone," is a famous John Donne poem. What he means is that nobody accomplishes their dreams all by themselves. We all need someone to help us get from where we are to where we want to be, someone to help us think our goals and processes through, someone to get feedback from about our work or our plans.

We need someone to believe in us and help us achieve our dreams. We are the ones who have to do the hard work of accomplishing and taking the risks we need to achieve our goals, but we will need the advice, comfort, and sometimes financial support of others. For example, when I was contemplating furthering my dream as a nurse, my friends stepped up to the plate and helped to raise my son as if he was their own. They took him to school, he stayed at their homes, they fed him, and no charges were ever incurred. This is the kind of help that one may need on the road to success.

Don't be afraid to ask. Don't be afraid to be vulnerable. And don't be afraid to receive kindnesses from others. People like to give and will feel happy that they were big enough to help another human being. When you are successful, you will do the same for someone else, too.

Be aware that you'll have to deal with the good and the bad in people.

When you are attempting something new, let's say, meeting a new mate, you will find that you will meet some good candidates and some bad ones. It won't be your fault, this is life. Not everyone on this planet is evolved, and we're not always evolved enough ourselves to see what people are really like. So you would be fantasizing if you think that just because you're a good person, so is everyone else. You, like all of us, will get tricked, deceived, and not treated the way you want to – in business and in your personal life. So what are you to do? Be attentive to who people really are, see if they walk their talk, and stick with the people you know to be honorable and dependable. Cut loose when you encounter someone whom you catch in lies or in dishonesty. They will not serve your success in any way. Forgive yourself if you get taken and move on toward your dreams and goals.

You do have to refresh your dreams.

Most of us are blessed to live longer than past generations have, not to mention people rarely stay in one job nowadays. That means most lives today include more than one career. Also, economies change, so the career we may have initially chosen might have become obsolete, and we now need to embrace a new path. Or we may find that we always dated one kind of man, and it never worked out, so perhaps we need to consider a new kind of man this time. The main thing is that we do not give up and we keep following our own star. We all need to take our experiences and keep refining what we want and keep developing ourselves toward more of what we want in our lives. We know what we are good at, we know what it is we are striving for. Now think about it in new contemporary ways and see how you can refresh

22

your dreams to be in keeping with the times, the new you, and new opportunities. We will discuss more of this in the principles.

So let's begin now with the principles of success. Apply these to whatever goals you are striving for.

PRINCIPLE #1

Identify Your Unique Purpose on Earth

"Many people are more comfortable with the expected, what they know. But that does not mean you should not blaze a new trail. That trail may one day be deeply valued and may be a sign of advancement. So always respect your adventurous, creative thoughts."

~ Norene Thomas

"The whole secret of a successful life is to find out what is one's destiny to do and then do it."

~ Henry Ford, Founder of Ford Motor Company

Our purpose is what feels "right" when we do it, what feels as if it was meant to be. As an example, I have no fantasies or beliefs in my being successful as a dancer. I know I have no talent in that area (although I love to dance). Success has to come from the deepest part of ourselves that knows where or how we have something unusual to give or say. Just like when you know a person is right for you, you can feel it in your gut right away. You can't talk yourself into loving someone, and you can't talk yourself into the wrong profession for you. We all have a purpose on this earth. For Steve Jobs, it was designing customer friendly technology. For Tyler Perry, it was making movies, not that both these men did not have bumps along the

25

way in their chosen professions. But neither gave up their professions when they came across those bumps, because they knew what their purpose was.

Divorced people often say that they knew on their wedding day they were making a mistake. That inner, still voice within us is very profound, some would say it is the voice of God. Others would say it is the voice of the soul. And then, there are those who will say it is their gut speaking. But whatever it is, it is the voice of truth and it knows where our success is waiting for us.

You are unique and your uniqueness is your success.

No two people are the same. We each have unique fingerprints and faces and we each have unique talents. That's why we should not get jealous of anyone's success, because someone else's success does not nullify our own. We have a different road ahead of us and we must walk our own road towards our own dreams and goals. Just because IBM was successful did not mean that Apple should not exist.

One writer does not nullify another's talent. One talented nurse does not mean another cannot be talented. One nurse, for example, may have a gift for diagnosis, another for patient care and empathy. Both are needed.

We can't waste our time fretting over other people's success, but simply focus on what we know to be our unique talent and figure out how to become successful at it.

Take responsibility for the gift of your talents.

Everyone has a specific talent, whether it is in the arts, management, or in finance or in health care or with people. You may be entrepreneurial, inspiring, motivating, or empowering to others. That talent is your unique gift and it is your responsibility to study and develop it. If you are good with people, perhaps you should be a mentor, a coach, or maybe even a consultant, and you need to study to be the best you can be. If you are talented at helping people, you might consider studying therapy or success counseling, marriage counseling, etc. If you are talented in management, you might want to be an entrepreneur or become a consultant. There is training for all these gifts.

The worst thing you can do is ignore your gifts. You will have a lingering sadness and regret inside you all your life. You have to be kind enough to YOU to give yourself a chance. Once you fulfill the path toward developing your gift, more and more opportunities will present themselves to you—offshoots of your gift—and you will keep developing beyond your wildest dreams.

We never stop growing, thank God. So begin your journey NOW to being who you really are. There is no time to waste. And guess what? When you are doing what you are meant to do, you will never work a day in your life. Why? Because you will love what you do. Sure, you will encounter difficulties and people who distress you and success not coming as quickly as you want, but you will love what you are doing and you will feel that your "inside" is in synch with your "outside."

There will be no inner conflict. You will be working with your God-given talents.

Don't be frightened to be a trailblazer by being yourself.

When you read the lives of people who have accomplished great things, many times people thought them foolish or did not encourage them. Many times it took years for them to be understood or heard. Many times people even rejected their efforts. Many times they were full of doubt. But they were blazing a new trail, and when you are blazing a new trail, people either aren't ready for the new or they don't adjust quickly. Many people are more comfortable with the expected, what they know. But that does not mean you should not blaze a new trail. That trail may one day be deeply valued, and may be a sign of much needed advancement. So always respect your adventurous, creative thoughts. Encourage the parts of you that want to go into new places, take risks, and try something new.

The world progresses through invention and invention comes from taking leaps into the unknown. Where would we be without those leaps? So say yes to that within you that has a desire for the new. You may be making new advances that are very needed and you can't see it just now.

Accept that doing something new may not be rewarding at the beginning.

Being a trailblazer means sometimes digging the trail for others to follow. It can often feel like you are working alone and you are going to have to wait longer for success. That may be true, but if you are a trailblazer, it will not matter that much. As Tony Hsieh said, stop chasing the money and start chasing the passion. Passion, if it's not momentary and just an idea, is always the right spur toward your purpose. Your purpose will take time and you will need passion to keep going when there is not enough money or you need lots of patience. Passion for your purpose is your rocket fuel.

THE GREATEST LOST AND FOUND

Interview with Forrest M. Willett on Passion and Purpose.

NT: To what do you attribute your success?

FW: I lost the most important person in my life in a horrific car wreck. It was not my wife or my son, I lost myself. I lost who I was as a husband, father, and friend. I lost my ability to read, write and speak fluently. I was a two-year-old child in a 31-year-old body. I could not even control my balance while walking. Just weeks before I had been a successful entrepreneur with offices in eight cities and 23 employees, now I was unable to even count change to buy a coffee.

A gentleman wanted to test drive a car I had for sale, I gave him the keys and I sat in the passenger seat and that's all I remember. Later, through the police investigation, it was revealed that the driver was speaking to his son on a cell phone and lost control of the vehicle at a high rate of speed. My first memories were 10 days later, waking up in the hospital. My wife Julie walked in to the hospital room with my then two-year-old son, Hunter. Although I recognized them, I was frustrated that I didn't remember their names. Although I knew what I wanted to say my no's were yeses and my yeses were nos. I would ask for cream but "coffee" was what I was thinking. People had a hard time understanding me and I had an even harder time understanding them. So for a long time I would remain speechless.

Through several MRIs and neuropsychological assessments, I was deemed to have a catastrophic brain injury. In a nutshell, I had a permanent loss of 55% or more of myself as a human being, mentally and behaviorally. An example of a catastrophic injury that would be easier to comprehend is the loss of two arms, two legs or both your eyes. I was in denial and in shock. How could I have lost so much? Looking in the mirror, and other than several scars and some broken and missing teeth, I was still the same person. I had to face reality. The reality was the things you take for granted every day, like getting out of bed, jumping in the shower, washing your hair, and brushing your teeth, were gone. I couldn't do it without the help and assistance of someone else. I was going to have to do something if I ever wanted to live a decent life. I attribute my current success to that horrific accident.

NT: What happened to your sense of self at that time?

FW: I had a whole team of professionals working with me daily, some of them were neurologists, psychologists, psychiatrists, surgeons, physiotherapists, speech language pathologists, occupational therapists, and the list goes on and on. Close your eyes for a minute and just imagine if you had a dozen or more of the top professionals in their field. whose full-time job it was to help you get from where you are to where you want to be, working with you and your goal tirelessly, day after day, year after year, and unfortunately you're still not reaching your ultimate goal. How would you feel? I started to spiral into deep depression and anxiety disorders, the feeling of hopelessness and helplessness was the flavor of the day. And my favorite activity became lying in bed all day in between my therapy sessions. I also became dependent on prescription medication, anti-anxiety pills, and painkillers such as Oxycodeine, Percocet and anti-depressants. Years later, I now see that the pain-relieving effects of such drugs also soothes the pain of a broken heart and broken dreams. I can also see how not having the ability to create a future can get people hooked on these drugs by chemically removing all fear and anxiety.

Catastrophic brain injury, clinical depression, several anxiety disorders, post-traumatic stress disorder, mild aphasia, and I could go on. I had many thoughts of, "What's the use? Why even try anymore?" I could not get excited about anything for the fear of failure was ever looming. I was a real mess. I felt like a puppet on a string being toted around by well-meaning doctors and therapist, do this, do that, try this, go here. And like a timid little puppy afraid of getting into trouble, I did just as they said, although I still felt as if I was getting nowhere until my favorite hobby of lying in bed finally paid off big-time one morning. I felt as if I had won life's lottery.

NT: What changed?

FW: We all have days in our lives that we will never forget, something so significant happens you remember the exact time and place you were, such as the day JFK was shot, or the day the Twin Towers fell on 9/11. My significant day came as I was lying in bed with the blankets pulled over my head waiting for the world to go away, when I heard the morning show host on television say, "Coming up next is Jack

33

Canfield with his new book, The Success Principles: How to Get from Where You are to Where You Want to Be." In my head I thought, "This is probably more crap," until the commercial was over and they introduced Jack. He claimed that his book, The Success Principles, could help transform anyone. It didn't matter what your current circumstances were, or your past situation. If you apply these principles, he said, you will transform your life. I have to say for the first time in years I sat up and pulled the covers off my head. I remember the words clearly that Jack said, "If you could do anything in life and there were no limitations, what would you do?" I remember chuckling to myself and thinking if I could do anything in life and there were no limitations, "I would take my two biggest disabilities and turn them into assets. Not only would I re-learn to read and write, I would become a best-selling author, and not only would I learn to speak fluently again I would become a professional speaker." I then chuckled again thinking "Yeah, right." Then I called my wife to come into the room and write this guy's name down, because I wanted to buy this book.

Julie looked at me, confused, and said, "You can't even read your son a night time story, how are you going to read such a book?" Julie entertained me and brought me to the bookstore to purchase the book only for one reason: she said she had not seen me that excited about anything in years. I finally had that spark back in my eyes. That was until I presented the book to my speech therapist, and told her that if I read this book and applied these principles I could write my own book, and become a professional speaker. I don't know if she was gasping or choking when I told her my exciting news. She explained a few

34

roadblocks I could run into, such as I could not read very well or comprehend what I was reading. Another roadblock was the immense size of this book, over 450 pages. The children's books I was reading at the time were 8 to 12 pages, and it took multiple readings for me to comprehend them.

My speech therapist and I made an agreement that I would give myself one year to read this book, and if I did not finish the book or gave up due to difficulty, that I would not beat myself up emotionally as I'd done in the past. I was now motivated more than ever not only to learn how to read and comprehend, but to show everyone there is life after brain injury and depression.

NT: What was your most important takeaway from the book?

FW: The first principle felt like a kick in the stomach: Take 100% responsibility for your life. The concept of taking 100% responsibility for my life did not kick in for a few months, until my son's birthday, when I discovered that baseballs don't bounce. (The title of my first book.) One of his friends gave him a present and as he ripped the wrapping away and threw it on the ground his face lit up with excitement. He was given a big white baseball in a black leather glove that looked four times too big for his hand, yet he was still excited. He dropped the ball to the ground and looked at it confused, he then picked it up again and dropped it. At that point his friend shouted "Baseballs don't bounce!" Those three words hit home very hard. I had to go in the house as I broke down crying. Here was my son growing up, and someone else had taught him how to skate and ride a bike. I was

35

missing his childhood while I was hanging out in the Ain't It Awful Club, telling all the Poor Me stories. At that moment, I realized I had to give up all my excuses and take 100% responsibility for my life if I was to get where I wanted to go.

Over the next week I did a really big life review, going over areas in my life that I had not taken 100% responsibility for and there were many. For starters, my family and then my rehabilitation. I would lie around in bed all day waiting for the therapists to show up and "make" me better, not realizing that I was to do the work, especially while they were gone. Somehow I just thought that it was their job to get me better. I realize now that was not the case. Just as Jim Rohn says, "You can't hire other people to do your push-ups." It now totally made sense to me that if I was to be better, I was the only person responsible for that, not my family, not my therapists. Me. It was time for me to get down to work and escape this self-created prison I was living in. It was time to "Take action."

NT: What other principles helped you?

FW: There are so many Success Principles that have made massive changes in my life. Principle number 15: Experience your fear and take action anyway. This one principle would help me overcome so many limiting beliefs and roadblocks in my life. I was at the point where I would not go out in public or speak with people that I'd known for years. I would have to take anti-anxiety medication just to go outside, that is if I wasn't too depressed to go out. So I decided to go out in public and start volunteering. My occupational therapist set me up with her friend, who ran the recreation department at a retirement lodge where I met many wonderful people. Tim Nesbitt was one of the first people to introduce himself, and we have since become close friends. We were both born in the same week in the same town, exactly 50 years apart. Tim was a proud World War II Air Force veteran. As I got to know him, he revealed to me that he had suffered through many of the things I had, such as depression and post-traumatic stress disorder. It was a relief to know that I wasn't alone. Over the next several years, I would spend three to four hours a week with Tim, and the more we spoke of how we felt, the better we both felt. When I first felt the fear and anxiety of going to volunteer. I backed out several times. I am so glad now that I felt my fear and took action anyway. Whoever would have thought that I would talk my way out of depression? In those early days of volunteering at the retirement lodge, I thought it was going there to help people. As it turns out, they were helping me. Tim really taught me how to be a class act even though he was retired and 93 years old. Every day he was well dressed and clean-shaven. He once told me something that will stick with me for the rest of my life, "When you make agreements keep them."

NT: What's another principle that helped you?

FW: Principle 13: Take action. The March of Dimes is an organization that helps many people with physical and mental disabilities. They were having their annual conference, and one of the speakers backed out so they asked if I would be willing to share my story of success and triumph over adversity. Although I agreed, I thought in my head; "Oh my God what have I gotten myself into. I am not a professional speaker and I only have 10 days to prepare." It was time for me to "act as if." This was my big chance to reach one of my biggest goals in life, and I wasn't about to let it slip through my fingers. I prepared a speech on paper with the help of my speech therapist, and read it over and over again for several days. On the day of the speech, I walked into the convention center to see a room of 287 people. Sweat rolled down my back like an April rain shower and then I stood up at the podium. My hands were shaking so badly I could not read the paper, so I set it down, took a deep breath and said to myself, "This is it, I am finally here." I looked around the room and started with a joke. I told the crowd that I was shaking so badly I could thread a sewing machine while it was running. Their laughter put me at ease and I was able to share my story without the paper. After it was over, I received a standing ovation. I had never experienced that in my life. It was a rush of feelings that I cannot explain. After the talk was over, I was approached by several people who wanted me to speak at their organizations. I was on cloud nine. Just a few short years ago I could not speak fluently, or put a full sentence together that made much sense, and now people want to hire me to speak all over the world. Wow.

NT: How did you transform yourself from essentially wounded to healthy?

FW: The greatest transformation in my overall well-being came from applying three principles together daily. Principle number 11. Visualization. Principle number 22: Practice persistence and Principle number 23: Practice the rule of five. Through my recovery, one of my

38

biggest obstacles was fatigue, the feeling of constantly being tired. This affects every aspect of your life, from relationships to your work life and your everyday well-being. The reason I was fatigued is that I was getting very little sleep at night, tossing and turning and worrying what the next day might bring. I was sent to do overnight sleep studies in the hospital on three occasions, and each time the only result was heavier prescription sleeping pills. I turned this around by making a list of my top five priority actions that I would do toward my goals the following day. I would then visualize the whole next day as if it were a movie playing in my head, the actions I would take, the activities I would be doing. It didn't happen overnight but my sleep improved tremendously over the coming months. I did have a slip up as I began to slack off on the visualization and rule of five, thus falling back into my old sleeping patterns. It was then I realized that I had to practice persistence with patience if I wanted the change to be long-term, and I did. As my sleep improved, so did my relationship with my wife and son, and when that happened I no longer felt as depressed. I went to my doctor with the goal of getting off the medication that I was told that I would likely be on for life. I exchanged the pills for exercise, diet, and applying these Success Principles. I have been off all medication completely since August 2007 with no symptoms of depression or anxiety, and I am still happily married.

NT: So committing to success principles is how you became a successful author and speaker?

FW: Building houses for most of my life, I know that a solid foundation is the most important part of a solid home. If you don't have that, everything else is out of whack. When I hit rock bottom I needed to start over, and The Success Principles were the solid foundation on which I rebuilt my life, and an extraordinary one at that.

Tips to Finding Your Purpose In Life:

1. Take a long walk or sit on a beach, and think about what you consider your greatest talents.

2. Imagine living out your talent and committing to it. How does that feel?

3. Do some research on people who have chosen the same purpose in life. Read books about them. Talk with them, if you can.

4. Commit to your talent and make it part of how you will achieve your success goals.

5. If your talent is unusual, don't be frightened. Don't focus on what has been done before but see what it is you want to do.

6. Make a plan for your talent. How can you develop it? Take classes.

7. Discuss your vision with a professional coach and see what insights that coach adds to your vision.

Questions to ask yourself about finding your purpose in life:

1. What would you consider your purpose in life and when did you know it?

   _____

   _____

   _____

   _____

   _____

2. How do you put it into action as a career for yourself or as a lifestyle?

   _____

   _____

   _____

   _____

   _____

3. Where do you take risks of not being accepted by the collective?

   _____

   _____

   _____

   _____

   _____

4. What is the price you will pay for following your purpose or dream?

_____

_____

_____

_____

_____

5. Define your purpose and write down people you admire who have similar purposes.

_____

_____

_____

_____

_____

6. Can you either read about them or get in touch with them to ask for guidance?

_____

_____

_____

_____

_____

7. What will you gain by following your purpose?

_____

_____

_____

_____

_____

8. How can you educate yourself more to live out your purpose?

_____

_____

_____

_____

_____

9. What help do you need from others toward living your purpose?

_____

_____

_____

_____

_____

PRINCIPLE #2

Only YOU Can Make It Happen

"Successful people get to it now. They can't get to it fast enough. They are consumed in what they have to do and they think about it all the time"

~ Norene Thomas

"Success usually comes to those who are too busy to be looking for it"

~ Henry David Thoreau, New England Transcendentalist and author of 'Walden Pond'

Now that you know your purpose, there's only one person who is going to make your success, and that is you. Nobody can do it for you. A journey of a thousand steps begins with your taking 100% responsibility for the journey. Your financial or business or personal success all depend on you saying to yourself what it is you want, and then clearing the decks to go for it, and going into continual action. You have to open the door to your success and do the work that gets you there. It is much easier to apologize for not getting there than to give yourself permission to go for it. You won't be a successful writer unless you write. You won't be a great doctor unless you go to school. You won't meet the right guy unless you get rid of the wrong guy. You won't get financially solvent unless you look at your spending and at

47

ways to increase your income. You won't have money unless you learn about financial accrual. You can't be an entrepreneur until you start your business. You are the one who is going to have to begin that journey of success and put one foot in front of the other toward your success. You will hire the coaches to help you, the experts in areas where you are weak. You will be the one to keep your shoulder to the wheel. You will be the one expanding your mind constantly. You will be the one building the blocks toward it.

The time is now.

We all fantasize about success. We will make a movie, we will be an actress, we will be a singer, we will start our own business, we will get married – you name it. And then, for some of us, we watch the movie and that's all that we do about it. We will get to it one day. But successful people get to it now. They can't get to it fast enough. They are consumed by what they have to do and they think about it all the time. They don't want to dream about something, they want to do it and see what happens. Success is not in your future. Success is in your present. Now is the time to begin, to be working at it, to be laying the groundwork. There are always obstacles along the way so, if you start now, you will experience prosperity and happiness that much sooner. There is no right time. There is just now and you doing all you have to do to achieve it. All you need to do is begin.

You already started by reading this book.

If you've picked up a book on how to get to success, then your mind is already working, already curious and open to success, and you've started your journey on the road to success. Picking up this book shows you are ready to learn, you are looking for tips. You are engaging with the part of yourself that has the success gene. So give yourself a pat on the back and know that you have begun. Know that you have taken the first step. And believe me, each step will be almost as simple as reading this book. It requires effort to read this book, make notes, and plan your strategy. But it is not impossible to make that effort, and it is energizing. You will find every step that you take will require strategizing and stick-to-it traits – all of which will be enlivening and fascinating.

What do I mean by 100% responsibility?

What does it mean to be 100% responsible to your success? It means educating yourself in your chosen field – with a coach, with a school (if need be), with books that will guide you (like this one), with seminars, or with friends who are success driven. It means being clear about where you want to go and taking the steps, not talking them. It means giving up the idea of being "saved," and replacing that with getting excited about "saving" yourself. It means becoming acquainted with self-esteem and pride in your efforts. It means being surprised at how the universe will work with you if you put in the work. It means stepping up to your vision and doing all that it takes to achieve it, 100% wholeheartedly. If you are only 20% responsible for it, you will only get 20% results.

Take complete responsibility for all of your actions, good and bad.

Make time for your success.

You have a lot of work in front of you. Whether it's analyzing your finances, or building a business, or becoming a coach, or buying a house – whatever it is, it will take time and focused hours. You need to make sure your schedule includes that. You can't go to the movies every night if that is your time for studying. You have to put the time in at your desk, no matter what career you are about to engage in. So look at how you are using your time and make time for your dreams, purpose, and goals. Go over your schedule and see what you have to cut out, so you will have time to get from where you are to where you want to be. You can't be all things to all people – you have to keep your eye on what it is you are trying to accomplish. You will have to learn to say no to some things, so you can say yes to building what it is you want for yourself. True friends and allies will understand and admire your motivation. The naysayers? You will have to let them go.

We understand your hesitation; change is scary.

Changing your life – even experiencing the fruits of success or finally finding the right relationship – will bring change to your life. And that may be subliminally scaring you. You will have to develop new mental muscles. We all have images of ourselves that we have grown accustomed to over time, and those images will need some tweaking. If you become financially solvent, you will be more aware of how you spend money and may be less happy-go-lucky. If you meet Mr. Right, you may have to learn how to keep a home in a different way than you do now. If you are building a business, you may have to forego holidays and giving in to people's demands. It will be a new you, and that may be frightening. There is no question that to do something new, you are

50

going to have to learn new habits, and that can be scary. Accept that and don't be hard on yourself. It may take a while to get new healthy habits of success and you may slip every now and then, but just start again. We're all human, not perfect.

Surprise! You're going to love it.

Let me tell you a secret. You are going to LOVE your new, healthy habits. You will say to yourself, "Why didn't I do this before?" It feels so good to be doing the right things to lead you to your success. So know that whatever decisions you make to be responsible to your plans and dreams are good decisions. That these new changes to your behavior and ways of being in the world will pay you back tenfold.

You have to be willing to go through what it takes.

The path to success is not overnight. There is an old saying, "Every overnight success story takes 15 years." You will encounter disappointments along the way, a resetting of your goals to reflect new information you learn along the way. You will encounter rejection and you will encounter (at least most of us do) doubts and lean times. This is all normal. So you have to have the strength to just keep going. Winston Churchill, the stalwart Prime Minister of England during the Second World War, who fearlessly defended his little island against Hitler's machine and refused to give up when all the odds were against them, said, "If you're going through hell, keep going." The end is not difficult times; it is just part of the path to success. So be prepared for difficult days and don't focus on the negative moments, just change your thoughts to where you are headed. Ignore setbacks and just keep on going.

Conversely, sometimes you just need patience.

In addition, there will be times when you will just have to stand still for a while to get from where you are to where you want to be. Sometimes patience can be harder to achieve than energy to push. We all want everything NOW, but there are times in life that we have to wait, too. How do you know when to wait and when to push? When you've tried every avenue you can, just sit. Something will open up. It always does. As the song says, "When you have done all you can, you just stand."

HUMBLE BEGINNINGS LEAD TO GREATNESS

Interview with Dr. Gale E. Gibson, President of Essex County College, Newark, New Jersey.

NT: Tell me how you got started.

Dr. Gibson: I was raised in Barbados by my grandmother. I came to Brooklyn and went to school there. During my studies, I participated in an IBM program that fostered learning for underprivileged kids. After I graduated with a Bachelor's in Technology, I went to work for IBM but did not feel that was my real purpose.

NT: How did you find your real purpose?

Dr. Gibson: I went to work and decided to attend Medgar Evers College of the City University of New York. One day, a light bulb went off when I was talking to my mentor. She said, "You don't always get what you want in the beginning. In order to learn how to get where you want to get, sometimes you have to stay where you are." So I stayed there 11 years, and became their founding Dean of the College of Freshman Studies, and Professor in the Department of Student Affairs and Services. Even though I did not love it, I learned a lot and it enabled me to get to the college where I am now the President.

NT: What happened?

Dr. Gibson: I started at Essex College in 2011, and after two years, the president decided to retire. I was appointed the new president and now I am in my 3rd term of a five-year appointment, doing what I love to do. I had always wanted to be president of a college.

NT: What do you think is the secret of your success?

Dr. Gibson: I knew I had to put roots down in the business I wanted to work in, and I was willing to take any position to learn and grow into it. I raised money for the school, and even did lecturing. But when the board was looking to elect a new president, they put out a search. They knew I lived and breathed the college, and finally decided to appoint me. We've been together a long time and I still love my job. That is what happens when you're living your purpose. It is not work.

NT: What are some of your high points?

Dr. Gibson: In support of U.S. President Barack Obama's national agenda for the community college, I became committed to pursuing initiatives to help low income and economically challenged students attain access to higher education. I was invited to participate in the white House College Opportunity Summit in Dec 2014, and I have participated in numerous follow up White House conference calls. As I continue to work with the White House, I am a strong advocate for the students of New Jersey and especially the students of Essex County College.

NT: What has been your personal charter at Essex College?

54

Dr. Gibson: I have been effective in saving the college close to $2 million in adjunct faculty expenditure due to scheduling efficiencies, while simultaneously building and deepening relationships with said adjunct facility. I have also been able to reinvigorate the college's academic leadership team with three academic deans, a director of academic assessment, an assessment specialist, and a faculty specialist. In addition, we have promoted and enhanced the institution's presence, academic programming, articulation agreements, and grant funding opportunities through community partnerships. It's been very exciting.

NT: Are you there to stay?

Dr. Gibson: I've been appointed as the seventh president and the second woman to lead the Newark-based Community College. I was selected to the school's top position by the college's board of trustees on October 15, 2013, after serving an extremely successful period as the college's interim president. That's because of my commitment to the college. During my tenure as interim president, the college applied for and was awarded over $24 million in grant funds which include $19.1 million from the state's Building Our Future Bond Act. These grants will be used to fund initiatives that will increase student graduation and retention rates, major campus expansion projects, new partnerships promoting urban farming and hydroponics, and a host of initiatives that will contribute to the overall success at Essex County College students. Of course I'm here to stay. I can't wait to see all these wonderful programs come to fruition.

Tips for taking 100% responsibility:

1. Sit down and think about what you need to do to achieve success in the areas you want to be successful in. Make a list.

2. Start taking action on each item. Figure out the timing of approaching each action item.

3. Visualize your success. What does it feel like to you?

4. When you are worried, look to your list and write out what you need to do. Focus on action, not worry.

5. Sometimes it will be tiring. Sometimes you won't get the results you want. Sometimes you just stand and wait.

6. Even so, make sure there is time in each day toward moving toward your success.

7. Don't talk about it. Do it. Say less about your plans and do more.

Questions to ask yourself about taking responsibility:

1. What does it mean to you to take 100% responsibility for your success?

    _____

    _____

    _____

    _____

    _____

2. What do you have to change in your behavior to achieve your success?

    _____

    _____

    _____

    _____

    _____

3. What steps are you putting in place to reach your goals?

    _____

    _____

    _____

    _____

    _____

4. Did you hire mentors?

_____

_____

_____

_____

_____

5. Write down an example of how you gave 100% of yourself to your goals. This will inspire you.

_____

_____

_____

_____

_____

6. How can you give more time to your goals?

_____

_____

_____

_____

_____

PRINCIPLE #3

Identify Your Goals and Make Them Tangible and Accountable

"We often have a resistance to writing down our goals, as if writing them down will make them smaller. Writing the, out and stating them becomes a responsibility. That is what is frightening us."

~ Norene Thomas

"Entrepreneurs average 3.8 failures before final success. What sets the successful ones apart is their amazing persistence."

~ Lisa Amos, contemporary singer

Identifying what exactly your goals are is the first step to moving things forward. In other words, knowing what you want is half the battle. You may want to be an entrepreneur but it only becomes real when you take action on figuring out specifically what your purpose and area of business will be, and how you are going to get there, market your products and get clients. Or, it may be that you want to have a meaningful relationship, so you need to identify what are the traits of someone you would like to spend your life with, and what kind of lifestyle would you like to lead. This will enable you to focus your sights on and recognize that kind of partner. If your current partner says he never wants to get married and you do, then, if you are serious, you have to look elsewhere. Since you now know your purpose, the

59

next step is translating your purpose into actionable goals. When I realized that I wanted the recognition of an RN as opposed to an LPN, I got to work and went about getting the proper accreditation and achieved my goal. I knew what schooling I needed and where I wanted to work. I made the outreach calls to find work where I knew I should be. So, this chapter will help you identify your goals and then show you how to live your goals in order to achieve them.

How to set goals. How to live them.

First you need to sit down and write your goals out for you to see and commit to on a daily basis. Don't be afraid to discuss your goals with people you trust. But be careful here to choose people who have your best interest at heart. Don't pick people whom you know are critical or negative. You need people whom you know have set goals themselves and achieved them, and who also have your best interest at heart. The reason you do this is twofold: one, it will make your goals more real and make you accountable, and two, these friends or associates may have some insights that will be useful to you. In fact, it is good to speak your goals out loud. There is a saying that the universe will come to help you, and I believe that is true. Let's say you want to start up a speech training business. Well, if you speak about it, someone may refer you clients unexpectedly, and so on. Now that you have written your goals down, make a list of ten ways you can move toward achieving them. For example, let's say you are starting a business. You need to make a Facebook page for it. Another action would be to investigate Google AdWords as a vehicle for marketing, and another would be making a website. Another would be sending out a mass email to everyone you know announcing your business.

Another advantage of writing down your goals is that you will find that now everything will begin to become part of your goals. Your conversations. The places you go to. What you pay attention to. You may be out with your spouse and suddenly hear something relevant being said at the next table. Maybe you will hear a videographer talking and so you will stop and ask about making videos about your business for your website. In other words, your goals will be with you all the time and your attention will constantly be on developing ways to move toward your goal.

Do something every day toward your goals.

Now you have your goals and a list of ideas to make them become a reality. The next step? Do something toward them every day. Do as much as you can. If you have a job and you are building a new business on the side, do something at night or on your lunch hour. Make calls. If you are in business and it is slow and depressing, reach out more. The best way to deal with difficulty is to fight it by taking action steps. Taking action will make you forget whatever fears or depression you are feeling. If you don't have a job and need one, apply to more places. Reach out more. Think of different ways to get your name out there. Ask friends to give you leads. If you are trying to get published and have many rejections, think of ways to publish yourself or start your own firm. There are endless ways of reaching your goal, so you need to be nimble to get there, and be constantly taking steps to try. If you do that, then you won't feel disappointed in yourself. And with every step you take, you will learn more about your goals and keep refining them to where you can be successful.

Your goals are your friends.

We often have a resistance to writing down our goals, as if writing them down will make them smaller. The real resistance in us is to bringing out front and center what is in the ether of our minds. Writing them out and stating them becomes a responsibility. That is what is frightening us. And of course all of us fear failure. But the only failure is not trying. There is no one who has not experienced hardship and frustration as they approach their goals, but the feeling of accomplishment that comes with each little step is something not to be missed in life.

As with all right actions, you will just feel better about yourself, you will increase your self- esteem, and feel in sync with your soul if you are moving daily toward tangible goals.

Take action on each goal.

Success comes from action, so you find me here repeating this thought. Forgive me but it cannot be stressed enough. Stars, successes in any field, got there through very hard work, as well as some failures. Sure they look cool as cucumbers on the red carpet, but they went through grueling auditions, sat in the cold for hours at shoots, and had to do the same thing over and over again. In other words, they were constantly at their chosen field. You must be, too. If you want to be wealthy, you need to constantly be working in areas that can render income. If you want to have your own business, you have to act it up, find vendors, find clients, and keep finding new and more clients. It never stops, and that is part of the joy of it. Your life will continually be creative as you do new things to make your goals tangible. Keep a notebook in your handbag or breast pocket, or use your smart phone, and you can make notes of new ideas as they come to you, to help you get to your goal, to help get you from where you are now to where you want to be.

Read about people who have achieved in your area.

Get biographies of people who have accomplished their goals in fields that are akin to yours. Then study how they did it. You will see that it took perseverance and an unwillingness to get derailed by difficulties. In other words, their burning desire makes them never give up. You will notice how they found people who joined them in their efforts, how they never left a stone unturned, how they finally got a break. That will be encouraging, motivating, and inspiring for you. In fact, make sure that each part of your day you are reading something that will inspire you. It will be fuel toward your success.

Spiritual books can also help, by calming the anxiety of starting something new and giving you courage. Books on Zen and meditation stress getting the chatter out of our heads and just being 100% focused on what we are doing, without an inner voice criticizing or distracting us.

Arnold Glasow started a humor magazine in the 1930s that he marketed to firms nationally, carrying this business on for sixty years. He published his first book at 92, "Glasow's Gloombusters," and was a real American thinker, self-effacing and generous of spirit, shunning the national spotlight. He once wrote, "An idea not coupled with action will never get any bigger than the brain cell it occupied.

Success is simple. Do what's right, the right way, at the right time." I interpret that to mean keep at it, and give your best to it. Success is not a result of spontaneous combustion; you must set yourself on fire.

GOAL SETTING IS FOREVER, NOT A PASSING THOUGHT

Interview with Dr. Selma Bartholomew, President of Legacy Parkways in New York (www.legacypathways.com), which is a consulting business working to improve schools, providing recommendations for and training in professional development for teachers, centered on improving content knowledge, pedagogy, and ways to help build relationships with students.

Dr. Bartholomew also works with the schools on curriculum development, goal setting, how to organize around these goals, and she helps schools manage the process of reaching their goals. Dr. Bartholomew's clients are nationwide, and range from the New York City public schools, to Catholic schools, among others.

NT: What are your specific immediate goals for yourself? And do you keep making goals for yourself?

SB: All the time. When you make a goal, it's not something you discard in a week or even in a month. It takes some real thinking on how much time you need to achieve a goal, such as a desired income, for example. I need to constantly be paying attention to my goal, refining it, keeping it front and center knowing it's a process to get there. I also need to know that there are always challenges and obstacles, and not to get disheartened by complex environments that make achieving the goal sometimes daunting.

NT: Is your goal setting a process?

SB: When I started my business, I had very broad goals, but as my business grew, I became more informed about what knowledge and expertise I needed to develop. I saw myself as a thought partner for my schools, and together we worked on growing their business, as well as mine, and that required goal setting that was strategic. My own personal goal is to constantly grow, and stretch myself so I always have goals that are about getting to the next level. Your ceiling must always become your floor. Your goal has to serve you and your desires.

NT: Are you rigid with these goals?

SB: Not at all. Flexibility has to be key because one is always getting new information and this refines your goals in new ways all the time.

NT: What happens when you don't meet a goal?

SB: No one meets every goal. It's impossible. They are roadmaps to keep us going. But when you don't reach a goal, have compassion for yourself, and know that what didn't happen this year might happen next year. If it is important to you and calling you, then put it back on your goals the next year.

NT: Do you make a list of action steps?

SB: Yes. Everything is within my hands. I am the one who chooses the sales number so I need to make the steps to get there. I also believe in personal development as I move toward my goals so I take action there.

Whom do I need to connect with? As an example, I have a new goal of writing about the philosophy behind my work. I connected with a coach and we are now on a book proposal. This is a new field for me and, once we get a contract, I will then need to hire people so I can become a speaker on the subject.

NT: How much of your time do you allot to achieving your stated goals?

SB: I assign different time frames to each goal. Some things take a year, others six months, others three months. You have to be realistic or you're just wasting your own time. I do not make unrealistic time allotments that are impossible to meet. Like to achieve something major in three weeks.

NT: What is your biggest resistance and obstacle?

SB: It sometimes feels like you're continually starting over. But one just has to accept that, and keep working in the area that seems stuck. You often think you're not getting anywhere, but you don't see that you are getting somewhere. It's hard at times not to feel disappointed when you haven't yet achieved what you want, and you've been willing to sacrifice time, energy, and money to it. But be faithful. Everything always feels like it's not happening quickly enough. We all need to have some faith that time is working itself out. You have to accept that the lesson and the growth for you is in the struggle of reaching the goal, and that as you make your way over through that obstacle, you are changing and stretching.

NT: How do you define your goals for yourself?

67

SB: It has to be important to me, something that I am willing to sacrifice for. I need to really analyze how it will make a difference in my life, and will I get something in the long term out of it. Asking these questions means I will discover something new about myself. There has to be meaning to our goals, will it make a difference in the lives of other people and the children. Are we moving things along for everyone? If that is true, then one can have patience with whatever time it takes to grow and blossom.

NT: So you are always growing new talents?

SB: Goal setting should include one's inner voice, what is pushing inside you to come out. And whatever you achieve, you should protect it. If you want to lose weight, don't start knocking back the French fries. Take advantage of any new habits you have acquired. Goals are in a way a declaration of new habits to get to where you want to go. So protect them, even when you get there. Keep up the good habits so more growth can occur. You need to sustain whatever you have accomplished.

Tips to help you define your goals and take action:

1. Write down what success you want that is burning inside you.

2. Write down 10 ways to achieve that goal.

3. Write down four people who might be able to help you achieve that goal, who could provide you with information to make it easier.

4. Analyze the 10 ways you have listed and then put in your calendar a plan to change your behavior, the new actions you need to take.

5. Make appointments with the four people you have listed as helpful to you.

6. Don't procrastinate. Do it now.

7. Make part of each day solely dedicated to the new areas of success you are moving toward.

Questions to ask yourself about putting your goals into place:

1. What are your specific, immediate goals for yourself?

   _____

   _____

   _____

   _____

   _____

2. What is your biggest resistance and obstacle?

   _____

   _____

   _____

   _____

   _____

3. Who inspires you along the way when you're feeling like you're going nowhere?

   _____

   _____

   _____

   _____

   _____

71

4. Can you better parse the hours of your day to be more effective?

_____

_____

_____

_____

_____

5. Are your goals reflecting all your ethics, and your long-term goals for yourself?

_____

_____

_____

_____

_____

6. What is a personal goal you could add to your list that will expand you as a person?

_____

_____

_____

_____

_____

PRINCIPLE #4

Fear Is What Gets in the Way of Success

"Most of those negative voices in your head are the fears of other people you heard as you grew up."

~ Norene Thomas

"What seems to us as bitter trials are often blessings in disguise."

~ Oscar Wilde, playwright, novelist, essayist and poet,
Most famous for his novel 'The Picture of Dorian Gray'

The number one reason people fail in life is they give up. Just imagine seeing someone you care deeply about giving up on their dream, or even struggling temporarily. You know the feeling you get in the pit of your stomach. As long as you keep going, keep trying, keep picking yourself up and starting again, you have not failed. Just know you must always persevere because success will not arrive on your door step unannounced.

Failure is sure to happen, none us are exempt from it. However, the secret of success is stated in an unflinching motivational phrase that has molded nations, gained freedom for countries, and fulfilled many dreams. This phrase is: "Never give up."

There are some success killers out there. But if you want to be successful in love or your own business, you're going to have to kill

73

those killers, which are mostly negative thoughts in your head. Most of those negative voices are fears, the fears of other people whom you heard as you grew up. Napoleon Hill has a joke: **"The no. 1 reason people fail in life is because they listen to their friends, family, and neighbors."** What he's saying is that people are listening to other's fears and not their own expertise. So let's take a look at some other thoughts and beliefs that get in the way of your success:

Not having a vision gets in the way of success.

How do you get to Kansas if you don't know you want to go to Kansas? True, you could accidentally bump into it but, then again, it's more likely you'll never get to it at all if you don't know you want to go there. So we all need a clear vision of what it is we want: a marriage partner, finances that are sustainable, a career as a CEO of our own company. Whatever it is, we have to be clear that this is what we are going for and then build our lives around achieving it. Success takes focused drive toward it, and we have to know exactly what it is we are driving toward.

Believing in rejection gets in the way of success.

Every successful person has been told, "You can't do it," "Your best work is not of interest to us," "You're too old to switch careers." That line didn't stop Colonel Sanders., who had failed, at age 65, 1,009 times before succeeding. "You're too young to lead," didn't stop Presidents Kennedy or Obama or Senator Rubio. "You're not pretty enough to model," didn't stop Lauren Hutton, who never fixed that gap between her teeth. "You're not smart enough to pass the math test," but most of us have passed tests we thought we'd fail. Whatever it is, most of those "theories" of who succeeds and who doesn't have been proved wrong by history and by people who are interested in success. J. K. Rowling got 20 rejections for Harry Potter. We know where that ended. She is one of the wealthiest and most beloved writers alive. So don't believe in rejection. Most naysayers are usually people who have not been successful themselves. Believe in your success and perseverance.

Not facing what isn't working gets in the way of success.

Successful people have certain important traits and one is looking at reality. If you are not making ends meet in your chosen field, well, you have to change it up. If your boyfriend won't commit and you can, he's not the right one. None of us can get blood from a stone. Or to use another metaphor, the first step toward success is "not trying to get a horse to run that has a broken leg." You have to admit to what is not working and then get help seeing what could, in fact, work. Maybe your business needs a coach to help you see where you can find an unexplored avenue to make money. Maybe you need a love coach to guide you toward not sabotaging your personal life. Maybe you need help managing your finances or a mentor on being an entrepreneur. There is no shame in asking for help from professionals. All successful people do. None of us knows everything. So if an area in your life isn't working, the answer is not to work harder, it's to work smarter. So the first step is admitting, hey, I need to do something new. Maybe I should talk to someone about where I am blocked. That gets you closer to your success.

Lack of courage gets in the way of success.

Doing something new involves courage. Why? Because when you do something new, you are letting go of old behaviors. Sometimes we're more frightened of that than we are of failure. But courage feels good and victory over our fears feels even greater. So go forward toward the new. Get help to release what isn't working and get excited about learning what you didn't know about. Be open. Being open is thinking outside the box. Talk to new people. Learn what other people did to overcome their fears. They will give you courage. All of us feel good in our comfort zone. But we feel great when we break outside of the zone into somewhere more exciting and more suited to us.

Not taking risks gets in the way of success.

Yes, I know this is a bit similar to lack of courage but there is a nuance here. You can't be successful unless you DO something, take actions. You have to try. You can tell yourself, "Oh, I am too old to become a nurse," or "I don't know how to write a play," or "I don't know how to meet a good guy because there aren't any." But unless you try, you'll never know or succeed. What's the worst that can happen? You fail. But you will know you tried. So you have to risk success to get success. So think action, action, action toward your goals. Don't think "my couch, my couch, my couch." Think energetic progress to the good, as Confucius said.

Not taking on new challenges gets in the way of success.

What I mean here is that we have to be emotionally available to the unexpected, to what we don't know. Something new can disguise itself, at first, as not being right for us. But it's just that the new can feel uncomfortable and so we think there must be something wrong. I once took a job where I had to be all about facts and figures. I never thought I would be good at that and then I learned I could do it and guess what? I did it well and it also strengthened my other skills. So increase your skill base by saying yes to new things you have never done before. As Michael Bobak said, "All progress takes place outside the comfort zone." Don't say no to an opportunity just because it is a new type of venture for you. It may be just what you need.

Not recognizing that people are important gets in the way of success. We all achieve success through working with other people. And our success will be enhanced by valuing their efforts and their talents, and by treating them respectfully and appreciatively. Our success will be enhanced by being empathetic to them and helping out where we can. Our success will be enhanced by allying ourselves with people who are success-oriented themselves, and who have the drive to achieve their goals. They will have intelligent ideas for moving our own projects forward. If we are closed off and think we know everything, we will be missing out on many opportunities, and people will not trust us as people who can achieve success. So listen to others, respect them, and learn. It will be invaluable to your success.

IF AT FIRST YOU DON'T SUCCEED, TRY AGAIN

Interview with Gay Walley whose novels were not making money. It was a play and film that brought her success. She had to break through some negative thinking to achieve success.

She also makes her living as a writing coach/editor. She is at www.nycwritingcoach.com

---

NT: Did you have fear when you switched creative horses?

GW: It was strange, but no. I was asked to write a play and my book agent and friends said, "Don't do it. It's a waste of time." But something told me to do something new, rise to the challenge. I didn't listen to the naysayers or even my own fears of not being able to do it. So I worked hard on a new way of writing for me, and it was my play that catapulted my success so that my books eventually did begin selling!

NT: A play is still writing, so you didn't completely change your career.

GW: You're right. And I had always been inclined toward dialogue in what I wrote. Also, interestingly, when I was a young girl I wanted to write plays but I didn't believe in myself. Then a play came looking for

79

me, many years later. Proving the universe knows what it's doing even when we don't! But if I had said no to the call, I would have missed great pleasure and opportunity for growth.

NT: Did you have to get help writing in a new form?

GW: Yes. I listened to people's suggestions. I trusted what I believed in and listened to people I admired. They were enormously helpful. I stayed connected with people in the industry and learned from them. I didn't listen to people whose comments did not seem relevant or helpful.

NT: How did your play get picked up when you were an unknown?

GW: Great question. I paid a woman out of my own meager money to advise me on what to do, and she told me how to showcase a play. A friend helped finance the showcase, a director who loved the play took the play on for little money, and we went "up".

We got great reviews and a producer saw it and I began working with her. It all came from taking a risk.

NT: What about your novels? Do you still write those?

GW: Yes, even though they have not yet been financially viable, but I believe one day they will be, so I ignore the financial rejection and go forward. You never know how life will work out and you have to put the work out there and be ready for how things can change. I am also continually searching for new ways of marketing. I have a resistance to social networking but I hire experts to help me and try to keep an open mind. Sometimes it works and sometimes it doesn't, but that is the tweaking that is necessary for any business.

Tips for giving up your fear:

1. Ask for help from coaches or successful people about how to overcome your worries.

2. Make a list of the new things you will have to learn, and start taking action steps to learning them.

3. Be willing to be uncomfortable as you take a risk.

4. When in doubt or worried, take positive actions toward your success. Make it that you don't have time to be fearful!

5. Know that occasionally you will fail, but that is just a part of the process.

6. Be patient. Success takes time.

7. Look at all the different things you need to improve to reach your goal, and write down next to them the appropriate action steps.

8. Listen to what other people are doing and how they did it and look for areas where you can implement their success factors into your life.

Questions to ask yourself about giving up your fear:

1. What is your vision for yourself of success?

2. What is your biggest fear in going toward it?

3. What risks will you have to take?

83

4. **Who could you ask to mentor you?**

_____

_____

_____

_____

_____

5. **Who do you trust enough to ask for help?**

_____

_____

_____

_____

_____

6. **Do you confuse obstacles with failure?**

_____

_____

_____

_____

_____

7. **Who could you talk out your fear of failure with?**

_____

_____

_____

_____

_____

PRINCIPLE #5

Success Requires Creative and Positive Thinking

"People rebuild from tornados. People find a new way after a serious accident. Life is very regenerative. You will find a solution to how to achieve your success if you are open to it and keep trying."

~ Norene Thomas

"It is not the strongest of the species that survives, not the most intelligent, but the one most responsive to change."

~ Albert Einstein, who developed the General Theory of Relativity, one of the two pillars of modern physics

If you are not successful in your chosen area, it could be because you have a block. It is as if you keep hitting your shoulder up against a concrete wall, and can't seem to break through. If you are not making the money you need to be making, there is something you should be doing that you are not. You are most likely not opening your mind to some new ideas that will jump start you toward success.

Even when it looks bad, there is always a solution.

It can be very frustrating to not get to where you want to be. I know you are a driven person just by the fact you are reading this book. So perhaps you feel defeated at this point. Nobody understands how hard you've tried. Nobody understands how hard you work. Nobody understands how long you've worked on your success or how badly you want this. We do understand. That is why we say it takes a shift in approach and doing something new to get different results. There IS a solution. And you (and I) will come up with it. So don't lose faith. Nothing is hopeless. People rebuild from tornados. People find a new way after a serious accident. Life is very regenerative. You will find a solution if you are open to it. As the anonymous programs always say, "Don't quit before the miracle. It is around the corner."

If something is not working, analyze it.
So let's be pragmatic. Write down exactly where you think you are stuck. You may or may not be right. But give it a shot. Where does the problem lie? Now think about some ideas of what could be the solution. Should you be increasing possibilities for yourself? Changing the way you present yourself? Do you have a fear of managing finances? Many people even have a fear of being successful. Responsibilities frighten them. Or just the changes that success will bring on. Whatever it is, you need to bring it to consciousness.

If you refuse to look at it or talk about it, it may be an addiction. If you know you are mishandling your finances and hide it from people, there may be a behavior you are frightened to give up. If you are not getting involved when you want to, you may be doing something secretive that is pushing others away. You have to really look at what is not working and be honest about it. Tell someone you trust. A therapist. A dear friend. Someone you can talk to. A coach. And then start to deal with the reality of what is in your way, rather than going round in circles in your head.

Don't burn bridges. You may have to cross them again.

Frustration can make us angry. Disappointment can also make us angry, and we may have an inclination to just lash out at the person who has disappointed us in business or in life. Maybe your partner turns out not to be as intelligent as you had hoped. Maybe one of your vendors lied to you. Maybe someone you work with never gets back to you when you need them to. Fact is these same people may have a positive impact on your life when you least expect it. People you may not like at one job may lead you to your next job, or hire you when you start your own business. So the solution is to be polite with all people and treat them how you would like to be treated. Truth is, you never know who will be your advocate and your ally. So never show your anger and always give your best to everything you do.

LET THE REDEEMER OF THE LORD SAY SO

Interview with Paulette Zimmerman, Vice Prelate, Non-Profit Activist.

NT: Did you have an easy or difficult childhood? Why/why not?

PZ: My childhood was relatively easy, and I am grateful to my parents who devoted their lives to their children. I was born and raised in the borough of Brooklyn, and I am the eldest child of four daughters. At a very early age my parents moved from Bedford-Stuyvesant to Williamsburg to provide a better quality of life for their young family. My parents were hardworking individuals who believed that they had an obligation and a responsibility to give their children the best that they could afford. I rarely understood why they made the decisions that they made, because they chose not to discuss family matters with their children. However, when I became a parent, I had a new respect for parental authority and the decision making process that matures children to adults.

NT: Tell us about some past and present struggles you may have experienced.

PZ: My goal was to always do my best. Mediocre was not a part of my existence. I wanted desperately to prove that whatever I did exceeded the abilities of others. Some people interpreted that attitude as arrogance while others felt that it was insecurity. However, in my heart I knew that there was a force inside of me that would not allow me to stop unless I was convinced that I was at the top of my class, or the front of the line. Doing your best can be admirable. However, when your best is misunderstood, it can lead to a very lonely existence. There were times when I really wanted a close friend or someone I could share my ambitious nature with, but I always seemed to connect with people who were not likeminded. Therefore, what could have become a close friendship became a competitive relationship.

NT: What are your biggest life concerns?

PZ: I sincerely enjoy helping others, and I often find myself very disappointed when I need a favor in return and everyone I helped is too busy to help me. Financial independence has always been a major concern, because I have encountered a number of roadblocks when it came to financial matters, and it was a long, long road to recovery. Frequently, there were occasions when I got out of one financial hole only to find myself spiraling toward another hole that was deeper than the previous one. Education remains a life concern even at this time of my life. When most people have completed their educational pursuits, I am still seeking other educational opportunities. I feel that there is a connection between good relationships, financial independence, and education. Clearly, a relationship can become very unstable when one partner reaches out to others, resulting in considerable sacrifice at home, and damaging the harmony within the household.

NT: How did you get from where you were to where you are now?

PZ: Perseverance has been and continues to be the order of the day for me. I have encountered a number of stumbling blocks because I refused to believe that if you continued to do the same thing you would get different results. As a result, I have often found myself returning to a point of origin because I did not heed the warnings that I received along the way. In some areas, I am extremely proud of my accomplishments because I know that for me it has been a faith journey, and I could not have made it without the hand of God in my life. I often heard my mother say that she wanted her children to go to school and get a degree so that they would be able to take advantage of some of the better opportunities life has to offer. I can list a number of occasions when my educational accomplishments did not bear witness to my mother's pearls of wisdoms. On those occasions, I was actually embarrassed that I had attained this level of education and yet I made mistakes that would normally be attributed to an individual who was a high school graduate. I have also been the individual who had the education but never reached the opportunities that are afforded those who can break through the glass ceiling.

NT: What made the lightbulb go off?

PZ: There were occasions when I did not allow the lightbulb to go off and I paid for my delayed reaction. By the time I realized where I was in my journey called life I had made some twists and turns that should have and could have been avoided. At this time in my life I am seeing a brand new lightbulb that I have never witnessed before. Many times we operate at the level of a 40-watt bulb when we should be at a 60-watt bulb, and we lose out on so many opportunities for bigger and better things in our lives. There are still occasions when my lightbulb flickers, just to remind me that life requires that we stay on course. When we get discouraged, frustrated or annoyed, we have a tendency to stop right where we are, which is indicative of our lack of enthusiasm to move forward. Therefore, we have to repeat many of our life experiences for a second or third time, because we refuse to put in the extra effort that would allow us to advance.

NT: What were some of the challenges you had to overcome?

PZ: In many instances, I wanted to have some of the privileges of the "rich and famous" among my friends and family members. It always seemed as if they were moving faster, and doing better, and I wanted to enjoy some of the same opportunities. Recently, I had a discussion with someone about one of my challenges in terms of my employment, because I work for a nonprofit agency and my salary is very low for my level of education. I had to be reminded that I was where I needed to be to do what I need to do. If I have a ministry matter in most instances I can take time off. However, in a different work environment that is more demanding, I might be making more money but time off might be very difficult to get. We tend to look at our challenges as negative, when the reality is they are often positive because they open new doors for us.

One of my family members has a beautiful home, excellent job with benefits, and she had been able to do many of the things that I can only dream about. I had to come to the realization that this family member is not in ministry (I am) and she was willing to travel and put in long, long hours to get where she is (I am not). She made a lot of sacrifices to get an executive position that I was not willing to make. With this in mind, I came to the conclusion that I made my choices just as she made hers, and my choices were the right ones for me.

NT: How did you overcome them?

PZ: Preparing the responses to these questions is providing me with an opportunity to get to do an introspective study. I am learning about the limitations that I have and the realization that many of the challenges of my past are still challenges in my present stage of life. I can honestly say that I have a better attitude about my challenges, because in a spiritual sense I feel that what I am destined to receive will happen before my time on earth is over. On the other hand, there are occasions when I ask myself why I did not wake up sooner so that I could have accomplished more by the time I reached this stage in my life. Clearly, many of us are in the same situation as we look around at others and wonder what we have done wrong. The interesting thing about life is that even when we feel that we have failed, the reality is that we are exactly where we were destined to be, with the situations we were destined to handle.

NT: What was your most challenging life/career experience?

PZ: On more occasions than I care to admit I have come to the conclusion that I never achieved what I truly desired to achieve. I have met some wonderful people and many of them have been very influential in my life, but I never quite met the standard that I desired. When I look at my life experiences, I often feel that I did not put in enough effort and if I had tried just a little harder I would have done more. Although I am not a "start and stop without finishing" individual, I have the feeling that I could have put in a little more effort, or the outcome could have been different. In terms of my career, I often wonder why so many people that I know climbed the ladder of success while I feel that I am still sitting on the bottom rung of the ladder. Even though I have done very well, there are occasions when I feel as if I could have pushed a little harder or started out just a little sooner.

I have a family member who came from a very poor family when growing up. This man is now a husband and father, but because of the deprivation in his childhood, he is a great lover of expensive toys in his adulthood. Whenever he has extra money, it is invested in an expensive adult toy. I am aware that this attitude stems from the fact that he had very little as a child. However, that is not my story. I had a sufficient amount of everything, and I never wore secondhand clothes or "hand-me-downs" in any area. Therefore, it is frequently hard for me to come to an understanding about my level of success and whether or not there is still time to accomplish more.

NT: What is your favorite inspirational quote?

PZ: "Let the redeemed of the Lord say so, whom he has redeemed from the hand of the enemy." This religious quote always gives me comfort and lets me know that for every mountain in my life, the Lord has been there and He has never allowed me to fall into a place where there is no escape.

NT: If you could be anyone you want to be, who would it be and why?

PZ: I have often heard individuals say that they wish they could be one of their idols who are rich and famous. As soon as I hear that statement I am reminded of how many of the rich and famous have led very unhappy and often tragic lives. I think one of the best examples is the Kennedy family. I would never want to imagine myself as a Kennedy. The Patriarch of the family had a stroke and never spoke another word until he died, two of the Kennedy brothers were assassinated, one of the children had a fatal accident while skiing. JFK Jr., who was one of the most handsome men in the world, lost his life in a plane crash along with his wife and sister-in-law. Ted Kennedy's son had bone cancer, he had brain cancer, and he suffered through a very unfortunate situation in his public life, where one of his staff members died and his family never recovered. With this in mind, I came to the conclusion that I just want and need to be me. I think I am best at being the person that I am, and as a result of spending many years in this body, I know myself and I can continue to work on this person on a daily basis to be the best that I can be.

NT: Who is the person you have never had dinner with, but would like to?

PZ: I would love to have dinner with Michelle Obama. Her story about being the wife of the first black president, raising two daughters in the White House, creating initiatives that allow her to be her own person, and the fact that she is an attorney who has been content to put her profession on hold until she and her husband leave public office is highly commendable. I am sure she has had concerns about whether or not she had made a wise decision after going to law school and passing the bar only to find herself in the position of a stay-at-home mom. Should she have continued her career?

NT: What are some of your own questions that you ask yourself when it comes to you? What do you think everyone needs to know about you?

PZ: A major question I ask myself is: How and why was I called to ministry? There are no other women in my family in ministry, and my parents stopped going to church by the time I was old enough to understand what was going on in the church service. Someone my family knew always came along and offered to take me to church. Even when they chose not to go, I was there as frequently as possible, and I loved it. I was teaching Sunday school at the age of 13. I have held every possible position in the church from Sunday school up to and including the Pastor. Currently, I hold the title of Vice President, which is a Bishop. I think that people need to know that I am committed and devoted to ministry after 25+ years, and I truly love helping people and fulfilling the ministerial mandate on my life. My children were raised in ministry, and my son is also an ordained minister. My grandchildren are now being raised in ministry and my grandson is a very talented and up and coming musician in our ministry. When we begin life's journey as children, we have no clue about the direction we will take. It is amazing that by the time we reach adulthood we have had many challenges and opportunities to take the high road or the low road to fulfill the impossible dreams in our lives.

Tips on creative thinking in areas you want to be successful in:

1. Don't burn bridges. Stay open to people coming through when you least expect it.

2. Take a walk and reflect on where you are stuck and see if a new environment helps you look at a problem differently.

3. Go see a movie or read a book to open your mind and then come back to where you are stuck. You will have new eyes and perspective.

4. Don't look at being stuck as failure. It's just process.

5. Talk to someone – either a coach or someone successful in a different field – and hear how they solved a block.

6. Ignore the block and just do the right thing. Move toward where you want to be and the block may take care of itself.

7. Feel positive.

Questions to ask yourself about your creative thinking:

1. What road blocks are you facing right now in achieving your success?

_____

_____

_____

_____

_____

2. Do you have the courage to really admit to them?

_____

_____

_____

_____

_____

3. What are you planning on doing about these roadblocks?

_____

_____

_____

_____

_____

4. Do you need to change something? What is it?

_____

_____

_____

_____

_____

5. Once you make the change, what other changes do you see taking place?

_____

_____

_____

_____

_____

6. Do you need to talk to a professional to get help changing?

_____

_____

_____

_____

_____

PRINCIPLE #6

Hard Work Is Made Up of Persistence

"You see it in thriller films. The main character stays alive by never thinking it is the end, but by continually coming up with solutions. We need to do the same with our own goals. Keep finding solutions."

~ Norene Thomas

"I've not failed. I've just found 10,000 ways that won't work."

~ Thomas Edison, Inventor and businessman

It's pretty simple. And I've probably said it before in different ways. But the key to success is definitely staying the course. The road to success is fraught with all kinds of difficulties, and those who succeed are the ones who don't give up. You see it in thriller films. The main character stays alive by never thinking it is the end, but by continually coming up with solutions. We need to do the same. If something is not working, then think what you could do differently. How to improve the situation. Make a list of alternative ways to get to your goals. If your business is not making enough money, then think what you could do differently than you are doing now, but stay on point. As an example, book stores saw that they could not make it on books alone. So what did they do? They added in selling gifts and

103

cards. We always have to be on top of finding new ways to get to our goals and to enable our dreams to flourish. Persist.

Stay focused on your core genius.

Even though I said to tweak your strategy till you are close to your success, I do not mean throw the baby out with the bathwater. Stay in the field you are meant to be in. Stay where your main talent is and believe in it. Don't suddenly decide to become an x-ray technician if you are a dancer and not making enough money. Find a way to make more money as a dancer, not leave your core genius. Teach. Offer choreography skills to ad agencies for commercials. What are some ways you have not thought of where you could apply your existing and beloved talents? Whatever field you are in is where you have gained a body of knowledge, and that is where you should be focusing. Don't jump ship, just find ways to maximize your core genius.

What do I mean by your talent, your core genius? Tom Rath defines it as a natural way of thinking, feeling or behaving. He also describes investment as time spent practicing, developing your skills, and building your knowledge base. These become strengths and the ability to consistently provide near perfect performances every time. So stay with your talents and where you have invested time developing your skills.

Develop 5 new success habits.

If you are reading this book, then there are clearly goals in your life you want to bring to fruition. The difference between the past and the future will be the new actions you take. Think of five new success habits you can do that could result in positive outcomes for you. Exercising three times a week to keep you in physical and mental good shape? Staying in one night a week and solely focusing on your new business? Reaching out weekly to a marketing expert to promote your business? If you don't cold call and you should, should you be adding that as a new habit to your daily routine? Only you know what these five new habits should be. But you should do them habitually – not just one time. They should be as much a part of your daily living as having dinner. Look at the areas of your life you want to be more successful in and then think of five new habits you can implement that will help you achieve your goals. Pick five habits you have never done before. Then you can really analyze if they are making a difference.

Spend part of each day on improvement.

This is a little different than forming new habits. This is making sure you spend part of your day doing something that will make you smarter, more efficient. Something that will help your brain get closer to accomplishing your dream. So if your business is a little weak in social networking, spend a little time each day reading about it, and learning new trends and opportunities. If you are becoming a writer, make sure you are spending part of each day reading excellent writers to help improve your language. If your goal is to become an entrepreneur, study the techniques and journeys of other entrepreneurs, or see a business coach or take classes about starting your own business. You will be improving yourself by learning. Self-improvement revolves around doing something that will strengthen your knowledge in your chosen goal/dream.

Mix with and listen to other people who are interested in success, or who have achieved success.

There is nothing more inspiring than being with people who are driven, focused on their goals, and know what it takes to achieve dreams. There is an unspoken bond when people meet up who have done well. You know the expression, "Like goes to like?" It means that people of similarity attract each other. So if you are with successful people and listening, then you know you have the gene. If you are only with people sitting around shopping or watching television, then you are not in a dialogue that will inspire or enlighten you.

Successful people know people who can help you. They know how to make things happen. They know avenues you may not have thought of. They know how to be encouraging. They are happy, and happiness makes things happen. Happiness attracts people and ideas. Happiness believes in the future and the new. Happiness works out of kindness and love and the best parts of ourselves, and spreads love in the world. When that happens, good things happen. So always put your best foot forward, and bring joy to others and mix with those who also believe in that. That way things will ignite.

You don't have to take big steps, just a series of small ones.

Robert Collier, of magazine fame, said "Success is the sum of small efforts, repeated day in and day out." If our mind tells us we have to move half way round the world to achieve our goals, or we have to completely change our life, then we are sabotaging our success. Success is made up of putting one foot in front of the other, right now, right where we are. Woody Allen made the joke that half of life is just showing up, and there is truth to that. Go to that meeting even if you don't want to. Reach out even though you don't feel like it. Keep quiet at a meeting and listen to learn something new. Make a new contact. Take a small risk by attending a seminar on a subject you need to know more about. Hire someone to help you where you are weak. Whatever small step you take will, strangely, have big results.

GETTING A BUSINESS PARTNER DOUBLED THEIR SUCCESS

Interview with Joanne Naiman, a principle of Reasonable Divorce Resolutions, a divorce mediation company (www.mediate.com).

NT: How has persistence been part of your business?

JN: You need a lot of persistence. In marketing yourself, you have to be flexible; if one way isn't getting you clients, you go on to the next thing. We've redone our website several times. When you have your own business, you have two jobs: the work itself and the business of running your business. The internet opened up huge areas for us.

NT: What was one way you made sure that you separated yourself from your competition?

JN: One way was I started with a partner. I wanted to have more of a presence. I met my partner in training and knew we worked well together. At first I thought I would consult with her, but we were so good together, we decided to form a partnership. We are very alike in some ways, both responsible, time freaks, and almost organically know how to divide up the work we have.

NT: You are a bit in the vanguard in New York, where divorce mediation is still new.

109

JN: Time will catch up with us. One selling point for us is that we can negotiate a divorce agreement for about 1/10 the cost of settling a divorce by hiring two attorneys and litigating. Walk into a lawyer's office to get a divorce, and in New York you might be looking at a $25,000 retainer to start. We don't even have retainers. Our services are on the rise. People are seeing the wisdom in this saving and in a kinder gentler way of getting divorced. Other states mandate mediation for couples seeking a divorce, but that is not true yet in New York. In some ways mediation is a new vehicle. When I was in law school, learning to settle disputes through mediation wasn't even taught.

NT: What kind of marketing techniques do you use?

JN: We give a free consultation educating our clients on mediation. You need to do that in an infant industry.

NT: Were you using your core genius in developing this business?

JN: Well, I am formally a lawyer and also I have a very strong knowledge of psychology. Divorce mediation is sort of a blend of these two skills. I did not like being a litigator because one is constantly on the assault, aggressive, encouraging a take-no-prisoner's attitude. Divorce mediation is about de-escalating the conflict, which is worthwhile work. You're not just helping the people in front of you, you're helping their kids, who aren't going to be in the middle of an ugly divorce. This work is valuable for people and is true to our values.

NT: How does having a partner help you?

JN: Naturally there is a division of labor. But also we're both obsessional. So sometimes we obsess together to solve a problem, sometimes we take turns obsessing. But two brains are always better than one when we can successfully brainstorm together. We've been lucky that way. When things are slow or we have problems with clients, we encourage each other to keep going and to move forward.

NT: What other good decisions did you make?

JN: We made sure to really know our stuff. We are not the fake-it-till-you-make-it types. When we began, we found the best in the business mentor, and we turned to him for advice when we needed it. It cost us money, but it was an investment we believed in. We see that some people's separation agreements are really not up to our standards. We take seminars and keep up with all the latest information on divorce. We intend to be the cream of the crop in mediation and together we've put all systems in place for that.

Tips on how to be persistent to increase your success:

1. Make a list of five new habits needed to achieve your success. Book them into your daily schedule.

2. If someone has said no to you in an area you want to be successful in, ask again.

3. If one door has closed, open another one.

4. Keep looking at where you can improve what you are trying to accomplish.

5. Make friends with a successful person.

6. Plan your day in a disciplined manner.

7. Keep working at it, no matter what. There are no excuses.

8. Sometimes stop and think of what you HAVE accomplished and think about what you did to get there. It will help you in how you approach a new venture.

Questions to ask yourself regarding your own persistence:

1. What are five new habits you added to your life to achieve your particular goal?

   _____

   _____

   _____

   _____

   _____

2. What kinds of things did you do to improve yourself in your path to your success?

   _____

   _____

   _____

   _____

   _____

3. Do you believe that happiness generates positive results?

   _____

   _____

   _____

   _____

   _____

4. Did you make a conscious decision to stay with your core genius? How are you doing that?

_____

_____

_____

_____

_____

5. What are your thoughts on persistence? Can you work a little harder on most days? Give a little more time to your goals?

_____

_____

_____

_____

_____

6. When something goes wrong, how can you just pick yourself up and keep going?

_____

_____

_____

_____

_____

PRINCIPLE #7

Learn How To Handle Rejection

"Beautiful women get cheated on, brilliant people are often passed over because people are scared of them, educated people do not always get the job they want. To be alive is to experience love and success, as well as heartache and rejection."

~ Norene Thomas

"Success consists of going from failure to failure without loss of enthusiasm"

~ Winston Churchill, Prime Minister of England
during the Second World War

There is no one alive who has not experienced rejection. No matter how educated, brilliant, beautiful a person is, they do not always get a "yes." Beautiful women get cheated on, brilliant people are often passed over because people are scared of them, educated people do not always get the job they want. To be alive is to experience love and success, as well as heartache and rejection. So don't go around feeling you are a failure or ugly or doomed or worthless, just because not everything comes to you when you want it and how you want it. Life has many twists and turns, and it is your job to do your best, keep striving, be ethical, be unrelenting in what you are trying to achieve, and ignore the rejection, learn from it, and keep going. Nobody who has achieved anything has not experienced countless rejections. So you are not alone, and you are not unique in being told "no." So much of a "yes" is being in the right place at the right time, and these are circumstances you have no control over. All you can do is increase your chances of being in the right place at the right time, and you do that by not giving up.

Rejections are about the person doing the rejecting, not you.
We all take rejections very personally. But that is a mistake. If you do not get the job or position you want, it is about other people's comfort zone. They may have in mind a specific type of person or resume. This does not nullify your accomplishments if you don't fit their type. Plenty of great people have been rejected. Never does anyone remember the name of the rejecter. So don't take it personally. It could be the day the rejecter is having, personal biases, and nothing to do with you. Kafka only had two books out when he was alive, all the others were rejected. So many successful authors could make wall paper out of their rejections. Forrest Gump took 20 years to get made, so many people rejected it, and it went on to win many awards. So rejections don't always mean lack of success, they just mean some projects need more time.

How to ask even if you think you'll get a "no."
This is about courage. It is hard to get a no, but if you begin to realize that the no has nothing to do with you personally, then your feelings will be somewhat protected. It's just a no, not the end of the world. But

if you don't ask, you have no chance of getting a yes. We all so very much want to be taken care of and think others will intuit our needs and desires, but the fact is other people don't think too much about us, they think about themselves. So if something is very important, you need to ask. You may get a no, of course, but at least you will know you expressed yourself. Also, they may say no now, but later on, come around to a yes. So always ask, so people have time to adjust to what it is you are asking for. Most people need time to reflect alone and ponder. And if it's a real "no," then you can make an educated decision about your next move, which will be to keep asking until you get the answer you want, which is a "yes."

Sometimes a rejection may mean you need to evaluate.
Ask your friends or someone you respect if you are contributing to the "no." Are you dressing right for the interview? Is your resume presenting well? Does your presentation need more work, better visuals? Are there areas you could improve yourself BY GETTING HELP? That is how things can get faster to a yes. So when you get rejected, confer with someone you trust. Or ask why you are being rejected. If you get an answer that makes sense to you and is an area you can improve in, then add that to your list of action steps to help you get where you want to go.

Life can change for the better in an instant.
When you get a rejection, it can often feel like life is bleak. That you will not get what you want, ever. Like most of us, you may internalize your disappointment and anger towards yourself. "I am no good." "I will never amount to anything." But keep in mind that after six no's,

117

you may suddenly get a yes and then you will forget all the nos. You will only get the yes if you keep on trying and don't let the no's get you down. It just takes one yes. It just takes one man to love you. It just takes one person to like your work to hire you. I have a friend who wanted to teach school but she came from another country. Everywhere she went she was told, "You don't have experience in the U.S." Her friend told her don't worry, someone will eventually see you for who you are. Sure enough, she was on an interview and the interviewer said, "You don't have experience," and she said, "I understood, a school as good as this must want the best," and then they suddenly changed their mind and hired her. Partially because she handled the rejection so well. She was gracious and empathic and it was those traits that made the employer change his mind. So you never know what is going to happen, and things may change for the best in an instant.

BEING OPEN TO THE NEW HAS UNEXPECTED GIFTS

Interview with Katherine Sibley, Chair of History at St. Joe's College, Swarthmore, Pennsylvania. Author of three books on American History.

NT: What were the most difficult barriers to your career?

KS: I had a rather peripatetic career as an undergraduate, many different schools and majors, from liberal arts to secretarial; it took me a long time to figure out what I was doing! Another barrier has probably been my reticence to try new things (Biography? Do I do that? Editing? Do I do that?) But it has been fun to try and transcend these barriers.

NT: How did your childhood play into you selecting your career?

KS: I don't think it did, consciously, but my mother had a bookstore (which began in our house), and there were many, many books at home, and I read a lot. Being that she was a war bride (she met my Dad in World War II) and her past was often swirling about us in her discussions and remembrances (1920s and 1930s England, for instance), it is likely that whether I realized it at the time or not, I became attached to the past and the legacies for the present it offers. But my conscious attachment happened when I was a young adult in the 1980s; I became polarized politically and saw history as the

119

"explanation" for what was wrong in the world. I then became fascinated with it. Fortunately, in ensuing years I dropped the sharp politicization in which I had cast it; now I love history for how it explains the "*zeitgeists*"—the varying periods and their just as varied preoccupations and moods—of the past. The 1960s are a fun time to study for just that reason.

NT: What do you still have to face each day?

KS: Will my students engage and be enthusiastic about my lectures? Will they talk? Will they find some fun and some interest in what we're discussing and reading? Sometimes, it's a "tooth pull"—and I always think I could do better when that happens, the material is engaging, after all—so how can I reach them? The excitement when you connect and see their delight in the discussion is just incomparable.

NT: How do you "keep on trucking" to your success?

KS: The joy that comes with finishing—but the process too! For instance, though I hate deadlines, I have to admit they are helpful. How else would I be getting through my current project? Of course, it's also about not disappointing people who are counting on me. And seeing it all in print—that's nice. Of course, the journey is also enjoyable—it's a privilege, to do what I do. I am very lucky.

NT: What was a career high point for you?

KS: Appearing on C-Span's First Ladies series to discuss First Lady Florence Harding in 2013, and organizing a scholarly conference on the 1920s based on my last book, on the Harding-Coolidge-Hoover era.

NT: What do you most love about your career?

KS: The ability to learn; in order to teach, you have to sop up the story and the information, and it's such a delight! Also, I so love working with people, both students and colleagues, who enjoy history as much as I do.

NT: How hard is to juggle family and career?

KS: I find that family is a welcome break! But balancing my time can be tricky. The distractions of life, of family, of fun; these are wonderful. I am sure I could be far more productive if I was not so pulled about by these distractions! But then life would be dull indeed...so the bottom line is, it's a balance, and sleep can be too often squeezed into the low single digits.

NT: What challenges do you see coming up for you and how do you plan on handling them?

KS: I'm not sure at this point what my next book or project will be. I have some ideas, but they involve a departure from my usual approach and I have some trepidation about that! I will test the waters, gingerly...with assurance that whatever happens, it will be an interesting experiment! And of course, with my son's bar mitzvah coming up, the work/family balance is going to be only more precarious. Insanity, no question, in the near future.

Tips to help you handle rejection:

1. Know that the rejection was about the other person, not you.

2. Ask a friend what you could do better to achieve your goal, just in case there is somewhere you are sabotaging that you do not know.

3. Sometimes the "yes" takes longer to come than right away. Be patient.

4. Everyone has been rejected. There is no shame. Know that.

5. If you've had a bad day, give yourself a treat. If you're really down, see a movie. It will change your head.

6. Thank the rejecter. They will be impressed by you.

7. Rejections can change in an instant. Keep trying.

Questions to ask yourself about how you handle rejection:

1. Do you fall apart with rejection? Do you hide? Do you give up?

   _____

   _____

   _____

   _____

   _____

2. Have you researched ten people you admire and read up on the rejection they experienced?

   _____

   _____

   _____

   _____

   _____

3. Do you consider failure a sign that you are getting closer to your goal?

   _____

   _____

   _____

   _____

   _____

4. Do you feel failure is humiliating? Do you throw out all your good

    traits when you have a failure?

    _____

    _____

    _____

    _____

    _____

5. Can you try to see things in a balanced way? That to attempt

    anything has a 50% of failure? No shame in that.

    _____

    _____

    _____

    _____

    _____

PRINCIPLE #8

Being Comfortable is a Sign of Not Doing Enough

*"We're probably not as out there in what we want to do as we think.
It just feels that way because it is new."*

~ Norene Thomas

---

*"The greater the artist, the greater the doubt. Perfect confidence is
granted to the less talented as a consolation prize."*

~ Robert Hughes, American football running back for
the Arizona Cardinals

Unless you have a little fear in you or a little discomfort as you move forward into or try out new things, you are not stretching yourself enough. It's a little like exercising. If nothing is hurting, then you're not exercising hard enough. If you're not feeling some discomfort in making calls, reaching out to new people, in trying to build your business, in attempting to complete a project that you know is a reach for you, then you are not growing. For one thing, you will be mentally healthier if you are stretching your mind. Read books that require attention. Learn a new language or a musical instrument. It will make you more adept in other areas. If you know you are financially irresponsible, then learn about financial responsibility. Stop taking

127

taxis or give up something that you know is not essential. It will feel uncomfortable at first but it will lead you to the success of having more money. We all have something we don't want to do; we're frightened of or think we won't be able to accomplish. We may have been embarrassed to fail in front of other people, or we think we're being too "out there" in our thinking....but we're not. That is how people trailblaze. People admire people who take risks and even fail. They admire the energy and the courage. And we're probably not as out there as we think. It just feels that way because it is new.

Release the brakes.

What stops us is that we tell ourselves it's safer to take it slow, it's safer not to try, you can't fail if you don't try. But you also can't succeed if you don't try. So whatever is stopping you from moving forward, release the brakes. Stop all the naysaying and negative projections in your mind. Just do it, as Nike said. Go forward. Whatever you are dreaming about, pondering, wishing for, go after it. Even if you don't get exactly what you want, you will grow and move toward where you are meant to be.

Do new things every day toward your goal.

So you have written down what your goals are. And you've written down what action steps to take. Now start making those actions real. Make sure you do something every day toward the areas you want to improve in. They will add up and lead you much closer to your success. If you do something every day, it will become a habit and successful results will begin to overtake you. Stop talking about what you are going to do, and do it. You will be amazed at what success results you will see.

Hold yourself accountable. Have an accountable partner.

When you have decided what you need to be doing, tell someone you trust and ask them to stay on top of you to make sure you meet your challenges. Your accountability partner does not have to be your friend. They just want you to stay on track. Talk with them about how it feels to do something new, what your resistances are, where you need help. Maybe that person has something they need to be held accountable for also, so you can be their partner in helping them. But the main thing is to be honest and ensure stick to it-ness, with the help of someone else whom you have already made the first step in new behavior by talking openly about your plans.

You should talk to your accountability partner at least once a week. They call you and you call them on a planned day and time although, naturally, you can be flexible when needed.

Be open to new ideas that come along.

As you begin exploring and pushing yourself, new ideas will present themselves to you. Don't dismiss them. They may be exactly where you are meant to be. So write them down, too, and explore them. You just never know. Success comes to those who keep trying, who fall down when there is a bump in the road, but get back up again. You may encounter an obstacle you can't get around and you will have to face it straight on. When this happens, make sure you learn from it and do not make the same mistake again and again. Your mind has to be

129

flexible, attentive, and not frightened of the unknowns in our life. So always be open to new ideas.

Failure is the result of "not trying."

Picasso was a painter and sculptor who lived a long life into his 90s, changing style throughout his life, and always being inventive. His output could probably fill more than 20 museums. He once said, "Only put off until tomorrow what you are willing to die having left undone." He never wasted time. Went to bed early, got to work early. I think the saddest thing is to be on your deathbed and think, Oh I wish I had done that. As the Japanese say, Take rest after death. Jump in! Try what you want to do. If you want to see the world and you can't afford it, find out how you can work your way around the world. If you always wanted to be a ballroom dancer, start taking lessons. If it is calling to you, it's for a reason. There is something in you that is meant to explore whatever is nudging you in your life. Think about what you want to have accomplished in your life before you die and get started. You don't need to know the how or why. Just do it and all else will fall into place. This is not to say that you will not encounter difficulties, because you will. But you should always take steps toward accomplishing your dreams. There is a saying, "Dreams are just thoughts that are dead until acted upon." So pick up the phone or go to your desk and start moving toward your inner desire.

NECESSITY IS THE MOTHER OF REINVENTION

Interview with Anne Gibbons, cartoonist, graphic artist and graphic recorder in New York

NT: Tell us a bit about your cartooning career.

AG: I've been a graphic artist since the mid-80s. In the 90s I began making a living creating greeting cards, cartoons, and illustrations. Although I never got to do my own syndicated cartoon panel or comic strip, I was quite successful. The cartooning business, like so many, began to change due to magazines using more photos and more computer generated graphics, which they could get practically for free. I always believed in creating a life I love, and it's wonderful to contribute a weekly cartoon to the King Features comic "Six Chix" and to create illustrations for a few clients, but it's no longer financially viable to have such a narrow focus. I spent several years licensing images for products that might be put on mugs, tee shirts and other products, as well as began illustrating commercial websites. But I was starting to realize that I was getting far from my original goal as a cartoonist, to illustrate my own ideas. I was starting to burn out on the difficulties in my business, how hard it is to make a living and how much the business was changing.

NT: How did you get into graphic recording?

131

AG: A friend told me about visual recordings for meetings and speeches and other events. She had taken a weekend workshop and signed up with agencies that represent facilitators and event planners. Graphic recording, which is visually putting on paper or a blackboard what a speaker is saying, sounded like a great way to use my creative skills. It's a natural for a cartoonist. So I began to look into it, took a few workshops and an online course.

NT: Did it feel uncomfortable at first?

AG: I took a three-day workshop to get started. I felt anxious to be venturing out of the cartooning world, doing something totally new. I didn't know what to expect, since I had come from a creative background. But I met an illustrator who was coming from a very similar place, as well as a former art director and a graphic designer who were charting new paths. In fact, at the end of the workshop, they asked the one best thing we took away from the workshop. For me it was meeting the illustrator who felt like a kindred spirit, even though there was so much I learned there.

In addition, when I first started working at graphic recording, I was uncomfortable going into the business world. For me, I had never had to wear makeup or dress up, working at home all the time. Now I was drawing at the front of meetings and being seen as a professional. So I had to look the part. This was new for me, too, funny as it sounds. I had to get a refresher course in makeup and get some new clothes!

NT: What was most liberating for you in making this career change or add on?

AG: I had to face letting go of what wasn't working. Let go of the belief if I just worked harder my cartooning and other life would work, even when objectively it was clear, it wouldn't. It took me a long time to face the fact that I could no longer make it in such a speculative field. Most cartoonists have some other source of income, and I needed one, too. But once I saw a new way, it was freeing to go into graphic recording, with people of all ages from various backgrounds, a field that is cutting-edge, exciting, and unpredictable.

NT: Did starting something new at an age when others retire faze you?

AG: It was rejuvenating, and I noticed nobody cared about age. It is uncomfortable to be old enough to be your coworker's or employer's mother. I am working with young, vibrant people, so I decided to see myself as old and vibrant. I did not want to undermine myself and take on the projection of aging as a downward spiral into retirement and fading away. It's the kiss of death! People who love what they do tend to work as they get older because it makes them happy. And it's important to me to make more money. I have had enough of squeaking by.

NT: What have you seen about doing a second or third career?

AG: A challenge keeps you young. I saw that much of the saying "We're too old" is dialogue in our own heads. Now that I am involved in graphic recording, I see people my own age, transplants also from businesses that have become outmoded and gone, and they too have reinvented themselves. It is hard for older people in today's work climate since we did not grow up with computers, cell phones, and social media. It's frustrating and uncomfortable to have to always be learning something new, but I love learning and it's satisfying to tackle something new and challenging.

Tips for being on the good side of uncomfortable:

1. Don't think it's a sign that things are wrong. It just means you're stretching.

2. Do something new every day to get in the habit, even if it is walking a different way home.

3. If you are frightened of something, maybe it is calling you to do it.

4. Sometimes it will feel scary to stand up for what you believe, but it isn't.

5. When you think someone doesn't approve, it may just be their being quiet and thinking. You have to be patient to let people come to your viewpoint.

6. When you learn something new, it will feel uncomfortable, but that is just process.

7. Make a list of all the new things you want to do – toward your success and just things you would enjoy.

8. Being happy is also a way to the road to success.

Questions to ask yourself about getting uncomfortable in a good way:

1. What new areas are you pushing yourself in?

   _____

   _____

   _____

   _____

   _____

2. What are you learning right now that is new for you?

   _____

   _____

   _____

   _____

   _____

3. What area related to your life do you feel intimidated by?

   _____

   _____

   _____

   _____

   _____

4. **How can you jump into that?**

_____

_____

_____

_____

_____

5. **Write down five new things you could be doing to increase your chances of success or five new things you've always wanted to do.**

_____

_____

_____

_____

_____

PRINCIPLE #9

Character Is Destiny

"Breaking an agreement tells the other party that they do not matter to you, only you do. It tells people that you cannot be counted on or that you are not honorable. People will not want to do business with or be friends with someone like that."

~ Norene Thomas

"Try not to become a man of success, but rather try to become a man of value."

~ Albert Einstein

What we create is who we are. Donald Trump is an extrovert who likes a lot of attention. He, creates that world around him. He personally believes you can do anything you want, and he furthermore believes America can do anything, too. It is his character that is driving his campaign for the Republican nomination (as I write this). Obama is introverted, believes in law, and is a man of family. He faces his presidency judicially, trying to do the best for all families. He is not beloved by reporters since he is introverted and doesn't make for exciting copy. His presidency is about his character.

139

Whatever your character is – nurturing, honest, creative, driven, numerical, pragmatic – that is how you will run your business and love life. So if you want to know what your life is going to be like, look to your character. We bring on our consequences. If you are a liar, you will be tricked and lied to yourself, because you will attract that kind of a world. If you are interested in superficial matters such as celebrities and shopping, you will find yourself with those people. You may be happy with that, since that is your character. Your character is your destiny. If you are a quitter type, it is unlikely you will go the long haul of becoming a rocket scientist. If you are adventurous in character, you will choose a career that suits that such as an artist, or in travel. If you are a nurturer or interested in people's minds, you will choose medicine or the healing arts.

Your character will be why people do business with you. If you show character, meaning you show you are a person who lives by values and what you believe in, and those values are ones of discipline, honesty and kindness, you will find that your employees will be of a higher caliber. The good people will trust you and, most importantly, stay with you. Your clients will know you tell the truth and always deliver. Your reputation will grow. If you want to know someone's character or your own, notice how many long-term business or personal relationships you have. If you don't, then something needs to be looked at. If you do, then you are someone people want to be associated with.

New businesses make something unique. Once they do and it is successful, it gets copied. As an example, there are many places to get coffee, but we tend to return to the places where they care enough to make the best coffee or where they treat us with respect. So if your character is such to give others your best, both in what you offer and in how you behave, you can expect to achieve success.

Always be honest and a person of integrity.

Honesty is the best policy is an old maxim. Why? Because once you lie, people expect you to continue lying and never feel quite comfortable with you. Liars do get caught out. Life finds a way of arranging that. People want to trust whomever they are talking to or engaging with. Sure, people hold back on information out of respect for privacy, or we wait for the right time to divulge information, and that can be a wise decision. But telling an outright lie sets up a bad precedent.

Keep your agreements.

It is important to keep any agreement that we make. Our word is all we have. Once you break an agreement, it is hard for people to trust you to the extent that they will make another agreement with you. Treat everyone as if they are the most important person at that time. Make your word be your bond. Breaking an agreement tells the other party that they do not matter to you, only your concerns do. It tells people that you cannot be counted on or that you are not honorable. People will not want to do business with or be friends with someone like that.

There is another advantage to keeping agreements, a major advantage: you will respect and trust yourself. Your life will be orderly. And you will attract people of like mind who keep their agreements with you.

Be a class act.

That means in every aspect of your life. Dress well, it is an act of respect for others. Speak well and do not curse or insult people. Find straightforward and kind ways of expressing yourself. Don't attack. Look at your own behavior in a communication difficulty, before you look at another's.

Be generous with your time. Give to others. Think of others. Keep learning so you can share what you learn, and add value to every situation, be it in business or just socially. Look at your life as being one where you have been given the privilege of service to others as a way of celebrating life.

Raise the level in your field.

You will represent your industry, even if you don't realize it. So look at it that you must always give your best and keep your standards high. Don't cut corners, you must not try and trick the industry so as to get more from it than you put into it. Always be ready with your best ideas, your best vision, your most honest and dedicated self, and your intelligence and kindness. Make your ideas represent high ideals and express them everywhere: in meetings, in your offerings, and encounters. That is what leads the world forward.

Have gratitude.

Fact is you are healthy enough and enterprising enough to be reading this book. That tells me you have drive and are a person destined for success. Right away you should be grateful. Let us never forget for a day the people who are good friends to us, or loved ones who love us. Or people who help us. Or that we have been given the grace of being healthy. Or we have been given a vision of our success. We are blessed. Successful people are not people who sit around blaming circumstances. Successful people capitalize on what is working in their lives and are grateful they have those assets. Make sure you take time, often when you wake up, to say thank you and be grateful to God or the universe for your blessings. And it never hurts to say an extra special thank you to all the people who help you along the way. Your friends who believe in you. Your spouse. Your children. Your co-workers who make you look good. Be grateful and therefore great-full.

Give back whenever you can.

Christopher Reeve said, "Success is finding satisfaction in giving a little more than you take." Sometimes you will find in your business that you are only living on values, not profit. You may decide to tutor a poor child for free, or you may decide to give your time to a sick person when you really should be working. It may feel counter-intuitive at times. You really should be working, you tell yourself. But, in truth, what matters in life is how we treat each other and what we learn. So when in doubt, do the right thing for others first. Stay at your wheel of your goals, but always be ready to help a friend or person in need. In a strange way, it is part of your goals in that if you keep your

143

own self in good spiritual shape, it will help your entrepreneurial life and other areas of your life, too.

INTEGRITY IS THE KEY TO HER REPEAT BUSINESS

Interview with Sally Engel, Sr. VP-Investments, Certified Financial Planner and Wealth Management Advisor at UBS.

NT What part does integrity play in your business?

SE: I handle people's money so my integrity or honesty is the foundation that my business is built on. Unfortunately, in the financial industry, Investment Advisors are often making headlines due to their lack of integrity. Ideally, with better government monitoring and improved technology to help red flag these dishonest actions, there will be less fraud committed against investors in the future. For a Bernie Madoff to run a Ponzi scheme and go unchecked for over 40 years is a crime in itself.

As a young Financial Advisor (then called stockbrokers or Registered Representatives), managing anyone's lifetime savings felt like an enormous responsibility. Of course potential clients trusted the reputation of the firm I worked for as well as the training I received... still, I felt that I should have additional training to help clients make essential financial decisions. I knew early on that I did not want to "trade" securities for a living so my solution was to become a Certified Financial Planner. This entailed passing exam in various areas of finance such as Investments, Insurance, Retirement Planning, and

Estate Planning and adhering to a Code of Ethics that helped me develop a financial roadmap for my clients.

NT: What do you think is the main advantage of being ethical in your business?

SE: Clients trust me and often refer their friends and relatives. I am currently setting up college accounts for a third generation client. I can also sleep at night, and even in these volatile times feel that my clients' interests are well defined and of utmost importance. In 2008, my main responsibility was to convince my clients not to sell their securities, which allowed them to recover in 2009 and partake in the bull market that followed. Integrity is the foundation of my business but communication is also an essential element. The phone can feel very heavy when you have to discuss the value of a portfolio dropping, but that too is part of running an honest practice.

NT: In what other ways do you feel you go over and above the norm in your profession?

SE: There is so much that I cannot control as an investment professional (i.e. the market) that the framework that I build for clients is what makes the difference. For example, I have always been willing to discuss very difficult subjects with clients, such as savings, aging (Long Term Care Insurance), illness, estate planning (family dynamics, wills etc.) and death (burial expenses or end of life wishes.) We never know what can happen to us in life but to be as prepared as possible can make all the difference in living a good life. I am not paid by the hour, so spending much extra time to help clients organize their

146

financial affairs separates me from many other Financial Advisors. I also take the time to meet their other key advisors, such as their accountants and attorneys, so that we are all on the same page. The end result is that my clients feel that they are surrounded by their trusted advisors.

NT: How does working the way you do affect your business?

SE: After 35 years as an Investment Advisor, I have created a business that gives me a great deal of freedom. Since my approach is "long term investing" vs "trading," I do not have to stay glued to a computer screen watching the market. I also set up meetings with clients to review their performance, so it is easy to manage my own time. In addition, I have put together a competent team that supports my efforts.

NT: What personal traits do you admire in others?

SE: I think the traits I admire the most are the ones I have aspired to achieve: integrity, honesty, communication skills, intellectual curiosity, and a trait that is probably a gift that one has or may not have...the ability to truly care about others.

NT: How have you excelled in your field?

SE: If you read the financial pages, you might think that the people who "excel" in my industry are all young hedge fund managers making millions of dollars per year for themselves. I would define "excel" as having a solid book of clients that I know and care about. I have had a long and gratifying career as a financial advisor and have made a good living putting my clients' needs first. It is a wonderful feeling to have clients say "thank you" and to answer the question that seems to be coming up more frequently these days: "What are we going to do if you retire?"

Tips to ensuring a good character:

1. Mix with people of good character only.

2. Don't lie.

3. Be on time.

4. Honor your commitments.

5. Don't think of money first. Think of service. Let the money follow.

6. Be your real self at all times.

7. Always try to give more than you are asked to. Forward helpful or spiritual information to others.

Questions to ask yourself about your character:

1. What service or kindness could you be offering to others in your life?

_____

_____

_____

_____

_____

2. What part does honesty play in your life?

_____

_____

_____

_____

3. What personal traits do you admire in people?

_____

_____

_____

_____

151

4. How do you try to be a class act in your field?

_____

_____

_____

_____

_____

5. How do you raise the bar in your industry?

_____

_____

_____

_____

_____

PRINCIPLE #10

Success Leaves Clues

"One way to be successful is to surround yourself with the best of the best.

Even people smarter than you."

~ Norene Thomas

"You may have to fight a battle more than once to win it."

~ Margaret Thatcher, former Prime Minister of England

Success does not happen in a vacuum, or all of a sudden. It leaves a lot of clues behind. Clues such as:

* Being someone who works hard and perseveres.

* Having the trait of constant vigilance toward what you are trying to achieve.

* Being clear about what you want but also being flexible enough to capitalize on what does go well, and let go of what is not working. As an example, sometimes you have a plan but an even better plan may materialize from your plan than your original idea. Let's say you build

153

a web site business, but you soon find that customers are more interested in your search engine optimization capabilities. If that would be true, then you would tweak your business to go after more of that and spend more money promoting there.

Here are more clues that people who are successful leave behind them.

Follow people who are successful in your chosen field.

There is so much to learn from people who understand your field (and this is true for those of you who have personal goals, rather than business goals. There are people surrounding you who have worked on those same personal goals, and achieved them.) Make a list of people you admire in the work you are invested in, or in the goals you have written down. Read about them on the internet. Study them in the news (if they are in the news). If you are an entrepreneur, follow their company and see how they market. Perhaps even set up a time to meet with one of their staff to discuss (not if you are direct competition.) As an example, when I had the daycare business, I obviously did not talk to a competing daycare business, but I would talk to a daycare business in another town and learn what legal issues I should know about, what marketing issues, the offerings that were successful for them and what were not. This helped me devise my own strategy. So I always recommend you get information from those who have already tread the ground you are interested in tilling. Follow people who are doing what you do well, and see what you can learn from them. It will save you money by eliminating some mistakes you could make, and it will show you many new ways of looking at opportunity.

Get a coach.

Coaches can really help you focus your goals, focus your strategies and look at what is not working for you. We all need a trained outside perspective. We all need mentors and someone there asking us the right questions to open up our minds and to help us process ideas we may not have thought of ourselves. Few people would learn the piano without a teacher. So why do we expect to be an entrepreneur or change self-defeating personal patterns without some guidance? Coaches are trained to help you with your issues and will save you a lot of time in getting rid of behaviors that may be in the way of your success. They will help you adopt new behaviors and tools that will bring your success about more quickly.

Take classes.

To be successful at something, you have to be top of your game. So if you are becoming an entrepreneur, take some entrepreneurial classes which cover marketing, accounting, business development. If you want to be a sales person, take some sales classes to learn about outreach and increasing your odds of a "yes." If you want to be an actress or a dancer, you need to take a slew of classes to learn your craft. Dreams are dreams, but classes give you the truth about what you are after, show you where your talents and pitfalls lie, and how to get better in areas where you are weak. So think about what you need to learn (social networking? What careers are available for older people? How to meet someone without going on the internet?), and search for a class. You will save time as well as make valuable contacts. You might find a partner to go into business with, someone who has different gifts than yours. You might find a wonderful new friend. Your life will open up and good things will come from that.

Ask for help.

Nowadays we have Facebook contacts, linked in contacts, and big email lists. When you need to announce something, reach out to all these contacts. There may be a client base there or people willing to help you launch a new business or get more clients. I know a woman who started a presentation skills business (she was an actress) and she even got clients simply by talking to people on subway platforms, buses, wherever she was. Many of those people led to new clients. Unfortunately, people are not thinking about us and much more likely thinking about themselves, but if you ask them for help, they are almost always willing to help. Asking for help means being honest about your needs. For some of us, that can feel like begging or being humiliated but the truth is, everyone needs help and most people understand that. When you ask for help, you are also modeling for others how they can ask for help when they will need to, and they will be impressed by your directness and your self-esteem in being healthy enough to ask. All of us need to both give and receive. And we can only do that if we ask.

Keep your books straight.

You can't run a business or run a home, for that matter, unless your accounting and banking are straight. When you need to send out bills, send them. When you need to pay bills, pay them. When you need to employ people, fill out the right forms. Why do I bring this up? Because if you don't handle this properly, it will come and bite you just when you don't want it to. Put money you earn into your bank account right away. Stay on top of your finances. Always be honest about financial matters, both with your clients and the people you work with. That will increase the good will of your reputation and make you feel better about yourself. Don't cut corners. If you work by the hour for a client, be honest about your time. People know when they are being taken advantage of, and if you get a reputation for using people, that will cost you far more than the extra money you think you are making for yourself. People are honest with people who are honest, and that should be the business climate you work in.

Always be looking for new clients.

If you are an entrepreneur, never stop looking for clients. The fact is clients attrite, it is just the way of life. People move, or even simply want a change, never mind how good your service is. It is human nature. So don't take it personally. What you need to do is constantly look for new business. Once you learn how to do it, it won't be so annoying. Concentrate on ways to market yourself. Should you have a campaign on Facebook? Should you just have a great sign somewhere? Only you know what suits your business, but whatever it is, each day should involve some outreach to new clients.

Use quality professionals to assist you in what you cannot do.

One way to be successful is to surround yourself with the best of the best. Have a great accountant, not your brother-in-law just because he is free. Have a good lawyer, a good marketing person if you are hiring one. Buy your products through reputable people. Why? Because successful people will lead you to other successful people who are successful by keeping to reputable business and personal practices. So, if you are hiring a resource, find someone you respect and whom you know has good references. If you hire someone without that, they may be initially cheaper but you will end up simply wasting your money.

Take care of your health. Sleep enough, exercise and eat well.

Doing anything new and focusing on success requires energy. So you have to be in good physical condition. That means get enough sleep so you have the energy the next day to handle all the different aspects needed for your success. Exercise to release tension and keep your body in good shape. Not to mention, any discipline begets discipline, so if you stay in shape, you are more likely to be in shape in your business. Don't eat too much, because eating too much can be a sedative and you need to have your best energy for success.

Just as important, take time for yourself every day.

Take a walk to refresh your mind. Be sure to take a vacation, even if it is just a weekend away from your computer or time in your home town. All of that refreshes you and will result in new ideas and renewed energy, which will result in more success for you.

Don't tell yourself you have to be perfect.

"Have no fear of perfection. You'll never reach it," the brilliant Surrealist painter Salvador Dali said. It is true. So many people don't try because they think, "Oh I can't do it perfectly." There is no such thing. Every novel has a flaw. Every cleaner have clothes they flubbed up. Every concert musician makes mistakes. Some computers break down. There is nothing that exists that is perfect, so don't let that inhibit you. Focus on what you do well and strengthen that. If you are good with people and give a personal touch to your business, then focus on what you do well. Capitalize on that. That is your strong suit. Don't focus on being perfect in every area. It's, as Dali says, an impossibility. You are just being hard on yourself and that is not a clue for success.

SOMETIMES YOU FIND YOUR CAREER BY WHAT YOU HAVE TOUGHT YOURSELF

Interview with Kerie Boshka, President of AARK House Publishing, Connecticut.

NT: How did you come to what you wanted to do with your life?

KB: By exploring what made me happy. I always felt I would write a book, and so I did. I'm not one to take "no" for an answer. And if you know anything about writing, "no" is a very common term. I'm always trying to improve what doesn't work. This got me into self-publishing. I began learning so much through this process. The more I learned, the more I began to work with other writers, trying to help them overcome the obstacles they, too, faced in the writing and publishing world. Helping people has led me to be involved in so many different other things: children's books, youth groups, and I suddenly realized that all these different directions were actually leading me toward one place—starting a publishing house where I could publish a new children's series, for example, and other work I believe in.

As I began my publishing house I came to meet amazing people in writing and publishing, and this has led me to shape a business that feels right to me.

NT: How do you know this is your purpose?

161

KB: Because I always follow my gut and intuition, and this publishing business makes me happy. I face struggles every day, but deep down there is a peace through the chaos. I know in my heart that I'm being led in this particular direction. That's how I know it is right. Because I believe if you are following the path you were meant to live, you won't fail.

NT: How did you learn the business?

KB: I am a hands-on learner. I have learned that there is no such thing as being an expert at anything. If I waited until I had all the details, I would never get anything done. Until you jump in and get started, you really don't know what you need anyway. My main focus is finding the right people to work with. I'm someone who finds the right people and then I jump in. I learn as I do, using coaches and experts in areas I need assistance in, and work steadily with them. I do research in my own way.

NT: So you devise your own purpose out of your own self?

KB: Yes, I don't follow other people's lead; I am more of a self-thinker.

NT: Did you use a coach for anything?

KB: I used a writing coach for the first book I wrote. I didn't really know how to get started, but I knew I wanted to write the book that I wanted to read when I was going through a very difficult time, struggling to find my purpose in life. Thanks to hard work and an amazing coach, I was able to provide a lot of encouragement to others.

NT: Do you take care of your physical health?

KB: Yes. I am very driven. Some even say obsessive. I wake up at 4:00 a.m. every day and go to the gym first thing. I run ten miles every day. Well, Monday – Friday at least. I take the weekends off!! Ten miles was my goal. It took me a long time to get there, and now that I've made it, I actually enjoy doing it. So it's not as bad as it sounds. I usually go to bed between 9:00 p.m. and 9:30 p.m. so I get enough sleep—or I'm a total bear. I have three kids, so I am busy with them, too. I am very focused and try not to get sidetracked. I think I'm probably one of the most organized people on the planet. Structure and organization are lifelines to me!

NT: How do you select whom you work with, even if they are freelance support?

KB: I get a first impression and I trust my intuition. People I work with have to be positive, honest, up front and direct, and say what they think. These are the qualities I look for.

NT: When you don't know what to do, do you reach out to someone who could help you?

KB: I always reach out to people. I am currently looking for PR people to help my author clients. I have meetings, I contact people, and I search till I find what I need to know. And when I find someone I trust, I stick with them. I'm a fiercely loyal person.

NT: Do you take time off for yourself to renew yourself?

KB: Yes. Sometimes I feel guilty doing it. But in order to keep going, sometimes I have to stop and be a little selfish. I love to read; a book can sidetrack me for hours! I work out and sometimes I take a quick cat nap during the day. Drinks with neighbors and friends is always a good idea. I need to keep my energy high to keep building my business, as well as run my family. Sometimes that means stopping and taking a breath.

NT: What do you think is the secret of your success?

KB: My natural curiosity. I don't let fear get in my way. Most risky ventures look like they're going to fail in the beginning. It's natural for all of us to second guess ourselves or give up. That's why I am very selective with who gets my time and energy. I surround myself with positive people who encourage and uplift me. The right environment is key to staying positive and believing in my "crazy" dreams. I can never listen to my fear because that's when I start getting negative—and nothing good comes from that. We have to keep going. That eventually takes us where we're meant to go.

Tips to leaving your own success clues:

1. Pick reputable people to work with.

2. Focus on being in the best health you can be.

3. Dress well every day and look professional.

4. Get a coach to hone your best skills.

5. Take a class to increase your skill base where you are looking to achieve success.

6. Take time off to renew yourself.

Questions to ask yourself about your own clues of success.

1. Can you use a coach to help you in your purpose?

   _____

   _____

   _____

   _____

   _____

2. Are you taking care of your physical health so you have energy for your purpose?

   _____

   _____

   _____

   _____

   _____

3. When you don't know what to do, do you reach out to someone who could help you?

   _____

   _____

   _____

   _____

   _____

4. **Are you focused?**

_____

_____

_____

_____

_____

5. **Do you take time off to renew yourself?**

_____

_____

_____

_____

_____

6. **Do you trust your intuition when making decisions?**

_____

_____

_____

_____

_____

PRINCIPLE #11

Build Upon Your Success

"You need to market your success. Let people know about it. Don't be shy. People are drawn to successful people."

~ Norene Thomas

"A thinker sees his own actions as experiments and questions – as attempts to find out something. Success and failure are for him answers above all."

~ Frederick Nietzsche, German Philosopher who exerted a tremendous influence on Western thought

Eventually, you are going to achieve success in some area. After all, you have been working towards it with great diligence and intelligence. When you do start to see some inklings of results, do you just sit back and relax? Maybe for dinner or a weekend. But then it is back to making sure you stay successful. You keep working at your chosen field, or marriage or weight loss. You keep attentive to what you did to achieve success and then you see what more you can do to get even more results. You think of new products that your customers might want. You fine tune your exercise program. You found the right guy or girl? Now you work on your relationship and heart skills. You learn how to make whatever you have achieved function even better.

169

A success is a sign.

If one part of your life became successful, let's say your coaching business or your webinar business or your dancing class took off, then don't say, "Oh I think I'll start to offer Spanish lessons." Stick with what is working! Do other dance classes. Make yourself a brand in the area where you have achieved success. Build upon that. If you've discovered a winning formula, add to and enhance that formula. That means you increase your chances for your success to continue. What is working, do more of.

How to capitalize on your success.

You need to market your success. Let people know about it and you. Don't be shy. People are drawn to successful people. Look how the country, despite whatever misgivings they have about him, is listening to Donald Trump and Ben Carson (as I write this). Because they purportedly were successful. That's what people want to hear about. So don't hide your light under a bushel, as the saying goes. Talk about it, consider a PR agent to write about it, post about it, not in a boasting way but tell the world you have this service and people are enjoying it. They will, too. Promote what you do and expose what is working as much as you can. People are drawn to success and will investigate. People want to be with winners.

Keep adding great people into your life.

Part of your success may be growing or finding a way to make your business or world larger. That may involve adding new people to your life. Choose those around you well – from your real estate agent to your financier to your marketing person. Choose people who connect with you as a person but you can sense take pride in their work, too. Choose people whose word is a bond. Choose people whose sensitivity you admire. Choose to work with people you are proud to be around and from whom you will learn. There will be an exchange of strengths, and this will further your success as well. How do you know what those people are like? As John Wooden, the American basketball player and UCLA coach, said, "Things work out the best for those who make the best of how things work out." Choose people whose whole way of living is to make the best out of whatever hand life has dealt them. They are the ones who will have good ideas just when you need them.

ONE INTERESTING FEAT LEADS TO ANOTHER

Interview with Ken Sander, Senior Technology Correspondent
BigPictureBigSound, New York City.

NT: What did you start out as in your career? Road manager?

KS: First I was producing a show called Peace Parade, and it featured the kids from the Broadway show Hair. We did concerts on Sundays (which was their day off), at colleges around New England. We did that for about six months, and it was fun and paid well. Then we were approached by a veteran music business manager to put together a touring show of Jesus Christ Superstar. So we put together a really good cast and staged it with dramatic lighting and a killer band. We toured for about two years before the Broadway show came out. After that, I was sold on the road and became a road (tour) manager.

NT: Then you became a talk show host? How did that come about?

KS: After 10 years of touring, I had my fill of airports and hotels, so I thought to myself, while I might not have a lot to say I had a good way of saying it, so why not television? Over time I hosted 3 different shows, one of which was The Cable Doctor Show. By doing the show I learned a lot about technology and had a good following. Looking to expand on my credibility, I opened a service center with the same name.

NT: Did you enjoy that?

KS: After 10 years I had gone as far as I could with the TV thing, and in fact I was writing a technology column in Penthouse magazine, which paid well and gave me a more interesting perch than the television career did.

NT: And now you write about technology. You stuck to your core genius. How did you make that come about?

KS: Actually, Bob Guccione was a regular viewer of The Cable Doctor Show and he hired me to write for Penthouse. I was there for almost 11 years, and from that platform I was able to get a bunch of tech writing gigs that continues today.

NT: Are you glad you have such a varied career?

KS: Yes, it's been an interesting and an exciting life. I sometimes envy people that had one direction (like being a Doctor), but then I've seen, done and been more than most. That has been a reward in itself.

NT: Does it keep you young (yes)?

KS: Yes, that along with exercise and being emotionally open.

NT: Do you think your attitude was a big part of your moving from one adventure to the next?

KS: Well, yes, for better or worse, it's how I'm built so I embrace it.

NT: What do you think you'll get up to next?

KS: Don't know but I bet there's one more left in me.

Tips to building upon your success:

1. Think what you can do to enhance your success. A new product? A new way to get closer to your husband? What more can you do?

2. Tell people about your success. You will encourage them and enhance your own life.

3. Hire someone to promote you further. Make sure many people know about you.

4. Share your success by being with other successful people, and see what synergies you can create together.

5. See your success as a sign of your talent and stay in that field.

6. Let people help you if they offer.

7. Don't get lazy. Sure, take time off and celebrate, but go back to work as soon as you can.

Questions to ask yourself about building on your success:

1. If you have achieved some success, are you doing more of that activity?

   _____

   _____

   _____

   _____

   _____

2. Are you thinking of other things you could do that are akin to your success, and you can capitalize on that success?

   _____

   _____

   _____

   _____

   _____

3. Are you telling people about it, not in a boastful way but at least owning it?

   _____

   _____

   _____

   _____

   _____

4. Do you pat yourself on the back?

_____

_____

_____

_____

_____

5. Do you keep at it, knowing that success can also drift away if not continually attended to?

_____

_____

_____

_____

_____

PRINCIPLE #12

Success Has Always Been Made Up of Connections

"Put your best foot forward in life and also in social networking.
Your image comes across there, too. Be accessible but not too loose."

~ Norene Thomas

"I find the harder I work; the more luck I seem to have."

~ Thomas Jefferson, American lawyer and principal author of the
Declaration of Independence

In the old days, it was the phone, it was referrals, it was one-on-one introductions. Now, as you know, connections include the plethora of people through the internet. This is a marvelous thing because you can reach a wider audience of business contacts or even friends or romantic interests. Some of us are resistant to social networking, but it is just the way of the world now. Customers now look up on Google where to locate the services they need. They check to see what other people say about a vendor, so entrepreneurs need to stay on top of social networking and try to post information that is useful to their client base.

We all need to put our best foot forward in real life, and also on social networking. Even online, our image comes across. So we need to be accessible but not too loose. No one wants to do business with someone who has lots of photos posted of themselves drunk. Be professional and self-respecting in any posts you put on the internet. Here are some of today's ways of being connected.

Facebook if you are marketing.

There are specialists who know how to segment audiences on Facebook, so think about advertising there or at least posting about what you do. You will be amazed at how many people will learn about you. Also friends of mine tell me they have made friends of like mind on Facebook who bring much insight and new information to their lives. Facebook may have its up and downs, but it is a force of the internet and not to be ignored.

Google AdWords.

This is a good way to keep your site front and center, and bring more clients to your business. Use them; it is cheaper than traditional advertising and you will get just as many customers. People look for services on the internet, not through other means. They know it is faster and can be tailored to their area, and particular needs. Google AdWords will increase your visibility.

Have a website.

This one is obvious but websites are now as important as business cards used to be. Make sure you have one.

LinkedIn.

This is the business connection place and you should be here. You never know who will connect with you and you, can use linked in to hire or be hired. You can ask for advice on business issues you have – i.e., where to find a marketing person or someone to work on your technology issues.

Blogging.

Some blogs just take. Yours could be the one. It's about passion. Write about what you are passionate about. Also if you have a blog on your site, you give your potential audience/customer a sense of what you are like, what your values are. It's a way your prospects get to know you.

Where to raise money.

Magically, many businesses have raised money on the internet for their projects.

These sites will help you fund projects and businesses:
- Kickstarter.com
- Indiegogo.com
- Fundable.com
- Gofundme.com

These sites are for social programs and/or charities:
- Startsomegood.com
- Causes.com
- Crowdrise.com

All these sites take a portion of what you raise, but still it is a non-traditional way of raising money and can be a lot of fun to implement.

SOCIAL NETWORKING IS, ESSENTIALLY, IN OUR DNA

Interview with Judy Shapiro CEO and Founder of engageSimply, a content marketing technology firm designed to help consumers and brands connect over topics of interest (www.engagesimply.com)

NT: What made you start this company?

JS: I was frustrated that the art of marketing was getting lost in the heavy handed technological science of marketing that began to dominate the industry around 2010. While technology provided wonderful new capabilities, the technological complexity simply made it too hard to deploy and measure campaigns.

NT: Was it difficult at the start?

JS: Our goal was to create a coordinated approach to the technically complex job of content marketing, and we encountered three levels of challenges. Technology: While many technical capabilities existed, there were few coordinated technology solutions. It became necessary to spend a lot of time analyzing the space and the current players. Customers: Marketing was technologically overturned in barely six years. The last thing advertisers needed was more technology – they needed simple ways to plan and execute content marketing campaigns. But that required a sophisticated understanding of data, ad buying, and direct marketing. The learning curve for customers is steep. And more critically, identifying measurable and meaningful metrics is very difficult to do. Access to capital: The ad tech world is dominated by young CEOs who understand the venture capitalist way of thinking better than the marketing customers they seek to serve. As a result, they did a better job of getting investment. For me, it was a challenge to get VCs to broaden their perspective and understand that the art of marketing cannot be ignored when developing the science.

NT: What do you see for the future of business vis-a-vis social connecting on the web?

JS: Social has become a big tangled world of confused capabilities, encompassing social networks, influencer marketing, social media buying, and social listening/ sentiment platforms. People try and convince business to blindly sign up for platforms or services that promise to activate social audiences. That disjointed approach will give way to a campaign-based set of platforms that connect social campaigns to clear results you can see. Instead of paying for ongoing platforms, business can use campaign platforms to launch limited campaigns.

Creatively, social campaigns will revolve more and more around topics that are niche, and with passionate followings, moving away from nebulous "influencer" programs. This way social activity can be tied to specific campaigns with clear goals or outcomes.

NT: Did you feel ahead of your time when you began?

JS: I did sense that the impending digital advertising onslaught was likely to degrade user experience so much so as to make much of digital marketing obsolete. My fears were realized when in just 12 months from 2013 to 2015 – people using ad blocking software jumped from 54 million to 121 million. The number is expected to reach about 200 million by the end of this year. I was quite public about my concerns for the user experience amidst the ad onslaught all the way back in 2012, with an article in Ad Age called: "The problem with impressions" (http://adage.com/article/digitalnext/problem-impressions/238134/). It spoke directly about the unbridled technological disruption of good marketing practice like delivering welcome ads in context to a user's intent. But my fears went unheeded because lots of VCs were making lots of money off ventures that had different types of tech platforms for social or mobile or some combination of the two. VCs are still looking to invest in a specific part of tech-based marketing, ignoring where the real value is being created, and that is with platforms that let customers deploy coordinated functions. These will be the winners over the next five years. It is the focus of our venture.

NT: What do you think of Facebook? LinkedIn? and Twitter as business vehicles?

JS: Well utilized, these offer tremendous value to businesses as a way to communicate to interested customers or prospects. Key though is to understand how to best utilize these channels in an efficient way without it consuming too many resources. Too often, businesses will rush in and try to manage multiple social networks at once. That tends

185

to diffuse efforts and undermine results. Instead, decide which social network is best suited for your business and focus your attention on that channel alone. Once you have developed a strong enough following, you can consider expanding into other social networks. Key to successful social media marketing, irrespective of channel, is consistency of presence and engagement. Over time, your commitment to your network will reap rich rewards.

NT: What do you believe an entrepreneur needs to bring to the table in social networking?

JS: The most successful strategy for an entrepreneur is to be authentic and consistent in your dealings with your digital audiences. Here are some key tips:

- Never use social media for a hard sales pitch
- Always ensure that your posts are genuine and authentic
- Stay current within your area and share helpful information
- Be respectful of others and never lash out
- Remember to stay positive as your community grows

NT: What is the future you foresee and how are you set up to be part of it?

JS: While the past has been about cool marketing technology, the future is about efficient deployment. Our company name, engageSimply, speaks to the mission of our firm – making technology that allows business to engage with their customers – simply.

Tips to increase your social networking presence:

1. Have a website.

2. Post good pictures of yourself.

3. Be on Facebook.

4. Be on LinkedIn.

5. Blog if you are an expert.

6. Submit your blog to the Huffington Post. You never know.

7. Use Google Adwords and Facebook for ads. Hire social networking experts if you are not adept.

Questions to ask yourself about your social networking abilities:

1. Are you on Facebook?

   _____

   _____

   _____

   _____

   _____

2. Are you on LinkedIn?

   _____

   _____

   _____

   _____

   _____

3. Do you have a positive presence on the web?

   _____

   _____

   _____

   _____

   _____

4. Can you get people to write about you?

_____

_____

_____

_____

_____

5. Should you be doing a blog regarding your business?

_____

_____

_____

_____

_____

6. Is there something you can offer your potential customers on the net? Tips? Insights? Are you known as someone who adds to the discussion of the field you are in?

_____

_____

_____

_____

_____

Truth is, Life is Wonderful

"The world is a beautiful place with its oceans, mountains, views, lakes, and cities full of wonderful people ready to help you and enable you to follow your dream."

~ Norene Thomas

Truth is, Life is Wonderful

I sign my emails with my name and the tag line "Life is Wonderful." Why? A number of reasons. First, the expression itself gives people a lift. But I really do it because I believe the statement, Life is Wonderful, to be true.

By just following these few tips, life lessons, and principles we've shared together, your life can be wonderful. The world is a beautiful place with its oceans, mountains, views, lakes, and cities full of wonderful people ready to help you and enable you to follow your dream.

You will be happier about yourself as you develop new healthy habits. That will result in your attracting healthy people to you and that will be wonderful. You will feel in control of your life and be able to handle all the obstacles we all have to face, and that will be wonderful.

You will know how to make plans and execute them and that will be wonderful. You will know how to ask for help and the universe will rise to do so and that will be wonderful. You will know how to set aside time for your own growth and success and that will be wonderful.

And you will know that to give is the most wonderful action we can take and you will have received help and now can give help, too, to those who ask for it.

Life is wonderful when you are living your dreams daily. You will never feel you are working but you will feel privileged to live this life of joy and satisfaction. The net result of all the hard work you have done will be realizing Life is Wonderful. And why is that?

Because it really is.

Acknowledgments

My life's journey was in no way easy. There were many hard knocks along the way, lots of deep bends in the road, and oh yes, I fell down many, many times. There were times when I felt I could not make it, but there was always someone there to help me on my way.

In no way can I tell you about all of the pitfalls that I encountered, but I can tell you about some of the people that helped me GET BACK UP AGAIN.

Robert N. Davoren, for starters, my wonderful husband and friend, who always dared me not to give up no matter what. He endured the peanut butter sandwiches and hot dogs during my hungry school years, and babysat our son while I went to school. No, he was not a **_Stay at Home Dad_**; he went to work every day. Honey, for all of the sacrifices you made, for your endurance of me going to school nights and all day Saturday, for the many nights you slept on the recliner because there were too many books all over the bed, and for making sure I got out of the house on time every day. For all of these things I thank you, I appreciate you and, most of all, I love you.

To my siblings, thanks for always being there and encouraging me. Of course, you guys would at times say, "Boy, Tip, you still going to school? It's time to stop working." Or one of you might say, "You can't take it with you." Just know that everything that you said was

193

appreciated and taken to heart. I know it was all because you love me and have my best interest at heart and are concerned. But just know that at the end of the day; I had to do it my way. Thanks and I love you guys.

To my dear friends Betty and Donald Fleming; Linda and Sam Carr; there is no way I can ever repay you for all of the many acts of kindness, love and friendship that you have shown me through the years. You were there when I needed you in my personal and business life. I will always be eternally grateful, appreciative and thankful to have you as my friends and family.

To Lillian, (Sis), Slim and Ann; oh boy, where do I begin, you have always been there no matter what. I make the call and you say When, Where and What. I appreciate you and am very grateful for everything. Love you guys and thanks.

To my children, I could not have made it without you. You are the reason for my being and keeping on being. Just know that the world is your Oyster and I love you very much.

Little Frankie; thank you for all of your help with Math. Even when you would say "Grand Ma, I told you that last night." Love to all the Grand Children.